CONTENTS

---

by Dr. Gary Hanson, Associate Professor of Higher Education
and Assessment Guru, Arizona State University

Assessing Student Learning and Development:

A Handbook for Practitioners

Marilee J. Bresciani, Ph.D.
Carrie L. Zelna, Ph.D.
James A. Anderson, Ph.D.

NASPA

**Student Affairs Administrators
in Higher Education**

Additional copies may be purchased by contacting the NASPA publications department at 301-638-1749 or visiting http://www.naspa.org/publications.

ISBN 0-931654-32-7

PREFACE

The purpose of this book is to assist student and academic affairs professionals (e.g., cocurricular specialists) with specific techniques, ideas, and examples for assessing student learning and development in academic and student support services. This book is not intended to be an academic text; rather, it is intended to build on the research of the great assessment scholars and provide the reader with tips to move past his/her assessment "sticking point" and engage in assessment. This book provides a general overview of assessment and offers practitioners detailed examples of tools that may be used to evaluate example student learning and development outcomes, which can be adapted to various types of institutions and programs within different organizational structures and varying resources.

As you may be aware, it is often quite controversial for cocurricular specialists to enter the student learning conversation; thus, in this book we are not differentiating between the assessment of affective and cognitive outcomes for two primary reasons:

1) We are trying to avoid academic arguments over the delineation between affective and cognitive abilities in order to focus higher education professionals on better understanding their contributions to student learning and development.

2) We are embracing the Student Learning Imperative's notion that "the concepts of 'learning', 'personal development', and 'student development' are inextricably intertwined and inseparable" (Schroeder, Blimling, McEwen, & Schuh, 1996, p.118).

This book invites cocurricular professionals to enter into the student learning and development assessment conversation. Recognizing that many of the cocurricular professionals' constituents move in and out of their programs, these practitioners require creative ways in which to approach the assessment of student learning

and development. This book will challenge cocurricular specialists to take earnestly their "responsibility for fostering student learning, requiring us to think about student learning in new and different ways" (Schroeder, Blimling, McEwen, & Schuh, 1996, p.115) and to assess that learning and development in even more resourceful ways.

How to Use this Book

This book is for any student affairs or academic affairs professional with a desire to assess student learning and development outcomes in academic and student support services. It is intended to be a hands-on reference for practitioners. It is not intended to be an academic compendium on the scholarship of assessment or the scholarship of research. Therefore, it is most important that the reader review the "Overview of Assessment" chapter and the "Introduction to Assessment Tools" chapter prior to reading or referencing any other materials in the book.

Assessing Student Learning and Development: A Handbook for Practitioner's may serve as a practitioner's reference for cocurricular professionals who seek to measure learning and development outcomes for their unit. It will assist practitioners in understanding the important differences between measuring needs and satisfaction and learning and development. The book will offer specific examples of measurement tools that will be easily applied to various areas of student affairs and academic affairs support services in any type of institution.

This book may be used as supplemental reading in graduate level courses in Higher Education and Adult and Community College Education programs. While graduates often leave their Master programs with an understanding of assessment, they are sometimes unable to put the knowledge into practice. This book will assist professors in teaching assessment skills to these students in a very practical applied manner.

The Scholarship of Assessment

We wish to acknowledge and thank the great work of those who have taught us so much about assessment and thus have allowed us to write this book. You will see some of the citations of these great assessment scholars throughout this book. In addition, these scholars' works have caused us to think beyond the pages of their manuscripts, challenging us to apply their principals and theory in practice. We have learned so very much from them by listening to their conversations and by their helpful day-to-day advice. Thank you all—particularly Jo Allen, Tom Angelo, Chris Anson, Trudy Banta, Greg Blimling, Michael Carter, K. Patricia Cross, Deanna Dannels, Peter Ewell, Jan Freed, Gary Hanson, Alan Harrison, Susan Hatfield, Karen Helm, Mary Huba, Pat King, George Kuh, Marcia Baxter Magolda, Peggy Maki, Gary Malaney, Marian McCord, Marcia Mentkowski, Catherine Palomba, Ephraim Schechter, John Schuh, Charles Schroeder, Geoff Scott, Joni Spurlin, Linda Suskie, John Tector, M. Lee Upcraft, Doug Eder, and Nancy Whelchel.

Acknowledgments

We wish to thank our partners for giving up valuable vacation time so that this book could be written. We thank our bosses and our colleagues who held down the "fort" while we had the privilege to be away from work writing. In addition, we wish to thank all those practitioners who inspired these words and asked the questions, which moved us to hide away at Deanna Dannels, Karl Lehman, and Baby Island Girl's Ocracoke Island home, drafting what we hope will be a valuable resource to all who seek to assess student learning and development outcomes. Specials thanks to the content editors of this book, Dean Bresciani, Savitri Dixon-Saxon, Tom Shandley, Caryn Sabourin Ward, and Lisa Zapata. You all took this on in addition to your family and work responsibilities, you gave us great advice, and we sincerely appreciate it!

FOREWORD

by Dr. Gary Hanson, Associate Professor of Higher Education
and *Assessment Guru*, Arizona State University

Quality is on everyone's mind in higher education. Students want it, parents pay for it, and corporate businesses and industries demand it. Taxpayers and legislators expect public colleges and universities to provide a quality education in return for their financial support. Alumni and governing boards have the same expectations for private colleges. An important facet of this demand for quality is the expectation that students learn important knowledge, skills, attitudes, and behaviors as a result of attending college. Colleges and universities can no longer count the number of books in the library, brag about the average SAT or ACT score of the most recent entering class, or simply report the student–faculty ratio and the six-year graduation rate. The focus has instead become, "What have students learned?" and "What are they able to do with what they have learned?"

The quality of higher education is not only about the educational outcomes we produce, but also the educational process we use to achieve those outcomes. Is higher education effective and efficient? Do our educational programs make a difference in students' lives? Have we used our educational resources wisely to produce the intended learning and student outcomes? We cannot answer these questions without effective assessment.

That assessment should be a high priority is no longer a point of discussion. Most colleges and universities accept the fact that assessment is necessary. The more challenging question is how to do assessment well. During the last twenty years, much has been written about why we need to do assessment (Astin, 1991; Banta, 1993; Erwin, 1991; Schuh & Upcraft, 2000; Upcraft & Schuh, 1996), but much less has been written about how to do it and even less about how to use the results. In addition, much of the literature on assessment is divided between academic and student affairs. Yet, student learning is a product of what happens both inside and outside the formal classroom. Consequently, student and academic affairs professionals must collaborate to assess student learning and development.

Does higher education need another book on assessment? Yes, I believe it needs *this* book. The need to provide a common assessment language across student and academic affairs when combined with the need to involve wider participation in assessment throughout the academic community is a strong reason why this book is needed. Equally important is the need for common methods and techniques that can be used to assess student learning no matter where the learning happens. Common methodologies will yield assessment information that helps faculty, administrators, and student service professionals improve educational programs and services. Using and understanding assessment results will encourage important dialogue about the mission of educational institutions and how well the intended outcomes of higher education are being achieved by our joint efforts to facilitate student learning and development.

The authors of this book, Bresciani, Zelna, and Anderson, document why collaboration of academic and student affairs professionals is important, and they provide important strategies and techniques for doing assessment. When you finish reading this book, you will have a much better idea of how to manage the assessment process and how to accomplish specific assessment activities. This book is all about the nuts and bolts of doing assessment. You will learn how to evaluate assessment tools and instruments; create and use assessment rubrics; and conduct interviews, focus groups, and surveys. These authors share how they develop and use best assessment practices, performance indicators, benchmarking, and peer and external reviews to better understand student learning and development. The advantages and disadvantages of using electronic portfolios, institutional documents, direct observations, and national standards also are discussed.

All in all, this book is a great resource on effective assessment. Treat it like a good guidebook and consult it regularly for the wealth of tips and techniques it contains. These authors are experienced assessment experts, and their shared wisdom and experience are based on many years in the trenches of day-to-day assessment. Using this book will help you avoid many of the mistakes commonly made when colleges and universities begin the assessment process. Follow their advice, and you will reap the rewards that good assessment brings to your campus: a better understanding of what and how students learn, high-quality educational programs and services, and a very strong sense that what you do makes a difference in students' lives.

References

Astin, A. (1991). *Assessment for excellence.* New York: American Council on Education and Macmillan Publishing.

Banta, T. W. (1993). *Making a difference.* San Francisco: Jossey-Bass.

Erwin, T. D. (1991). *Assessing student learning and development.* San Francisco:

Jossey-Bass.Schuh, J., & Upcraft, L. (2000). *Assessment practice in student affairs: An applications manual.* San Francisco: Jossey-Bass.

Upcraft, L., & Schuh, J. (1996). *Assessment in student affairs.* San Francisco: Jossey-Bass.

CHAPTER 1

Introduction to the Importance of Assessing Student Learning and Development

Colleges and universities are expected to provide evidence to their internal and external constituencies that the quality of education and the student experience is commensurate with rising costs, with their statements of excellence, and with their desire to retain the competitive edge. However, the modern university in the 21st century may be judged by a new set of expectations and criteria that go far beyond traditional sources of evidence such as resources, library holdings, standardized test scores, student–faculty ratios, student selectivity, and four-year graduation rates.

The emerging indicators of institutional excellence and quality are linked to the direct evidence that student learning and development is occurring. To assess the quality of undergraduate education at an institution, we need access to multiple sources of information that together reflect students' involvement in learner-centered contexts. Such contexts allow the learner to develop the repertoire of skills, dispositions, and core values that are linked to engaged learning, liberal learning, and lifelong learning. We have at our disposal the best research, models, and practices to guide our thinking and program development.

Decades of cumulative research indicate that students respond to intentional activities that are linked to positive outcomes. We can amplify our research-related evidence by evaluating the processes and outcomes that underscore real-world programs. We cannot only speak with confidence about "what we do," but we can also discuss "how well we do it."

Despite the presence of many success stories that could serve as guides or benchmarks to colleges and universities, most would be hard pressed to provide a body of evidence that indicates that they are learner-centered and committed to positive student outcomes. Earlier, we made reference to the new expectations for the modern university in the 21st century. One of those is that various campus groups learn to collaborate on common goals and programs. Kuh and Banta (2000) suggest that successful collaborations to enhance student learning may depend upon the ability of varied campus groups to understand each other's assumptions, values, beliefs, practices, and models. The most important—and yet most underdeveloped—collaboration on many campuses is between Academic Affairs (especially the faculty) and the Academic and Student Supports services areas, or the curricular and the cocurricular.

On many campuses the cocurricular collaborations can range from those that are nascent and underdeveloped to those that are meaningful and productive. On the campuses where collaborations are underdeveloped, this relationship is often characterized by the following traits:

- different perceptions of roles and responsibilities,

- lack of a common language,

- a power differential that ascribes more power to one group,

- an emphasis on the cognitive realm versus the affective,

- allegiance to different professional organizations and cultures,

1

- different sources of revenue,
- one group perceived as "thinking" and the other as "doing," and
- varied sources of evidence that each group is producing student outcomes.

The issue then becomes how silos and barriers can be broken down in order to facilitate successful collaborations. However, the residual benefits of collaboration generally outweigh those associated with stand-alone efforts. The benefits have been summarized in the literature (Kuh, 1996; Love and Love, 1995) and include an improved learning environment, higher persistence and retention, enhanced communication, more collegiality, better campus relationships, more emphasis on diversity, and a more positive view of the work of cocurricular professionals. Such outcomes represent shared goals that can be maximized when faculty and staff commit to intentional efforts to promote student learning and success.

The Educational Resources Information Center Clearinghouse on Higher Education (ERIC, 2000), NASPA (The National Association of Student Personnel Administrators), and ACPA (The American College Personnel Association) initiated one of the survey studies that shed light on the national picture of curricular and cocurricular collaborations in May 2000. The survey examined nine areas, two of which are appropriate for this book: (a) the reasons that collaborations develop and (b) outcomes assessment of collaboration efforts. One hundred and twenty-eight (128) chief student affairs officers responded to the electronic survey (49 percent response rate).

Why Partnerships and Collaborations Emerge

Survey respondents were asked to identify which of four reasons might prompt institutions to engage in collaborations. Learning was identified as the most important reason (35 percent). Leadership that has the authority to encourage collaborations was next (27 percent). The presence of a collegial environment was selected by 22 percent, and managerial pressure and accountability by 16 percent. Finally, the student as a customer was added by 9 percent of the respondents. Kezar (2001) notes that in the study institutions that emphasized student learning were slightly more successful with cocurricular collaborations. Those with

three or more successful curricular collaborations were more likely to have cited collegiality or leadership as significant reasons.

The questions that often confront cocurricular professionals when they consider implementing new programs and initiatives may not be framed in terms of actual learning outcomes. Obviously there are student development initiatives like service learning and leadership development that lend themselves to the generation of learning outcomes. Moreover, some outcomes are realized successfully without collaboration with faculty or academic personnel.

Outcomes Assessment: Perception Versus Reality

In the aforementioned study, 45 percent of the institutions surveyed reported that they conducted outcomes assessment, although half of that number reported institutional effectiveness outcomes (as opposed to learning and student development outcomes). It may well be the case that institutions chose to participate in the survey because of the existence of structured programs and outcomes-related evidence.

The prevailing reality is that the cocurricular side has a history of using anecdotal methods and indirect sources of evidence. While such evidence is beneficial in the development of substantive research questions and can often provide a macro picture, it may fall short of allowing us to interpret information with confidence, to discuss the rigor of the research process, and to use feedback in a way that promotes program improvement. What is important is that cocurricular assessment allows a program to gather important information and feedback that otherwise may go unnoticed.

It is imperative that curricular and cocurricular efforts, both individually and collaboratively, continue to develop evidence of student learning to respond to external pressures for accountability and the internal pressures associated with efficiency, effectiveness, and program improvement. In their landmark publication *Assessment Practice in Student Affairs: An Application Manual,* Schuh and Upcraft (2001) present both the compelling argument and the strategic direction that should underscore the thinking and practice of cocurricular professionals. They present the blueprint for assessment that allows outcomes to be documented, thus capturing the critical impact of cocurricular programming efforts.

The Need for Conceptual Grounding

For many cocurricular professionals, their efforts have emphasized holistic student development, cocurricular programming, and student satisfaction. Their contribution to the cocurricular experience is often the critical point of transition for many students. Despite the perception by many on the curricular side that academic concerns, like student learning, are their sole purview, the reality is that many factors in the learning environment impact student success and development. Both curricular and cocurricular professionals can forge a renewed commitment to higher levels of student learning and development. An important starting place could be the development of a shared conceptual understanding that would underscore actual collaborative efforts.

One document that can serve as the philosophical and intellectual guidepost for cocurricular professionals first appeared in 1994 and generated considerable attention. Since the publication of *The Student Learning Imperative: Implications for Student Affairs* (ACPA, 1994), cocurricular professionals have tried in various ways to link learning outcomes to their more traditional activities. This powerful call to action represented both innovation and a critical challenge, and to some it did not seem to be a good fit into traditional structures. Thus it was immediately embraced by some, but held an arms length with skepticism by others.

The Student Learning Imperative

This document is based upon a set of assumptions that keep the attention focused on student learning and related outcomes. Among these are the following assumptions:

- The terms and concepts learning, student development, and personal development are inseparable and can be used interchangeably.

- Optimal benefits and outcomes tend to be realized under certain conditions like active engagement and collaboration with others on learning tasks.

- Environments can be intentionally designed to promote learning.

- The outcomes associated with a learning environment must be assessed systematically and the impact of various policies and programs on learning and personal development periodically evaluated.

- Cocurricular programs and services must be designed and managed with specific student learning and personal development outcomes in mind. In other words, they must become a learning-oriented cocurricular division.

What often has passed as global outcomes must now be written in language that translates into learning and development outcome-based assessment. Staff needs to be trained to conduct systematic evaluations of their programs and services. Each unit or program should develop an assessment plan.

When cocurricular professionals see their efforts as learning-oriented, they become part of broader institutional audits and strengthen their relationship with the academic side as each seeks to promote the institutional mission. The promotion of the ethos that learning is the responsibility of everyone in the university or college community promotes ownership, and ownership promotes a commitment to excellence.

Powerful Partnerships: A Guidebook on Successful Collaborations

In 1998, the Joint Task Force on Student Learning generated a report that made the case that "when everyone on campus—particularly Academic Affairs and Student Affairs staff—share the responsibility for student learning, we will be able to make significant progress in improving it." The title of this report is *Powerful Partnerships: A Shared Responsibility for Learning*. The document reflects some of the best vision, wisdom, research, practices, and models on what we know about learning.

The report offers ten principles about learning and how to strengthen it, and they are grounded in a call for deliberate action. Associated with each principle are a set of cooperative practices "that bring together academic and cocurricular professionals to make a difference in the quality of student learning, a difference that has been assessed and documented." It is this latter emphasis, on assessment and documentation, that elevates a program or practice from one that is good and noteworthy to one that represents a benchmark, a critical component in an institution's culture of evidence. Since the report commits practitioners to an examination of learning and learning outcomes, it aligns more easily with the work of those in academic programs. The document asks cocurricular professionals to realign their focus and their efforts and to build upon their current successes.

The ten principles are as follows:

1) Learning is fundamentally about making and maintaining connections: biologically through neutral networks; mentally among concepts, ideas, and meanings; and experientially through interaction between the mind and the environment, self and other, generality and context, deliberation and action.

2) Learning is enhanced by taking place in the context of a compelling situation that balances challenge and opportunity, stimulating and utilizing the brain's ability to conceptualize quickly, and its capacity and need for contemplation and reflection upon experiences.

3) Learning is an active search for meaning by the learner—constructing knowledge rather than passively receiving it, shaping as well as being shaped by experiences.

4) Learning is developmental, a cumulative process involving the whole person, relating past and present, integrating the new with the old, starting from but transcending personal concerns and interests.

5) Learning is done by individuals who are intrinsically tied to others as social beings, interacting as competitors or collaborators, constraining or supporting the learning process, and able to enhance learning through cooperation and sharing.

6) Learning is strongly affected by the educational climate in which it takes place: the settings and surroundings, the influences of others, and the values accorded to the life of the mind and to learning achievements.

7) Learning requires frequent feedback if it is to be sustained, practice if it is to be nourished, and opportunities to use what has been learned.

8) Much learning takes place informally and incidentally; beyond explicit teaching or the classroom; in casual contacts with faculty and staff, peers, campus life, active social and community involvements; and unplanned but fertile and complex situations.

9) Learning is grounded in particular contexts and individual experiences, requiring effort to transfer specific knowledge and skills to other circumstances or to more general understandings and to unlearn personal views and approaches when confronted by new information.

10) Learning involves the ability of individuals to monitor their own learning, to understand how knowledge is acquired, to develop strategies for learning based on discerning their capacities and limitations, and to be aware of their own ways of knowing in approaching new bodies of knowledge and disciplinary frameworks.

Assessment

Among the methods of assessment that are linked to exemplary cooperative practices are those that highlight learning experiences that emerge from curricular and cocurricular collaborations. The documentation of such results is needed not only to demonstrate that learning and student development have occurred, but also to often justify the continuation of innovation and non-traditional programs. Among the college or university programs that were highlighted in the Joint Report, several report multiple methods of assessment:

The First Year Experience at the College of New Jersey is a collaboration between General Education and Student Life that utilizes service learning as the medium through which students ask critical questions about complex social issues and interact with communities. Assessment methods include student service learning journals, feedback from community agency staff, and student self-assessment.

DePaul University attempts to ease the transition of incoming students by allowing them to choose between two writing-intensive interdisciplinary and experiential programs. Assessment methods include qualitative and quantitative pre- and post-test surveys, the College Student Inventory, focus groups, and the review of syllabi.

At the Wellesley College Center for Women students take courses and engage in research experiences for varying periods of time. Evidence of effectiveness is obtained from course effectiveness instruments, an annual survey of program effectiveness, a self-esteem measure, an alumnae survey, and focus groups.

New Century College of George Mason University coordinates collaborations, Partnerships for Active Communities represents a combination of courses and programs that integrate classroom experiences with experiences in diverse settings. Assessment consists of student portfolios, documentation of work in progress, and evidence of self-reflection.

The Western College Program of Miami University, Ohio, is an interdisciplinary residential college featuring a core curriculum in the liberal arts for the first two years followed by individually designed upper-level interdisciplinary programs of study and a yearlong senior project based on all four years of study. Some of the assessment projects seek to document program impact on students, faculty, and staff. Assessment methods include quantitative, nationally normal outcome assessment instruments, student interviews, free writing, focus groups, portfolios, and ethno graphics.

What stands out at each of these institutions is the blending of a philosophical commitment to being learning-centered, and the real commitment to develop a "best practice" that can be assessed and evaluated. The collaborative nature of the contributions from student and academic affairs assures a best fit for each entity. Both divisions work through and agree upon a common language and process while maintaining their focus on the student.

How do Curricular and Cocurricular Collaborations Promote Student Learning and Engagement?

Colleges and universities that seek to develop collaborations should be clear on their expectations concerning student learning and engagement. Before the concrete is poured, certain questions should be asked that strongly influence the structure and process of the collaboration. Examples of some questions could be: What information about student learning and engagement would be compelling? Are we focusing on the real issue or concern? Are the proposed activities that are associated with the collaboration linked to outcomes that are linked to the mission? Will the collaboration promote cross-functional or cross-disciplinary learning? Does the collaboration reinforce the institution's vision of itself as a learning and learner-centered organization?

We can conceptualize some of the very specific ways that we think curricular and cocurricular collaborations can promote learning:

- The feedback to and from students about their experience will be more thorough and comprehensive. We will be able to better combine students' self-evaluation of their own learning and

development with the outcomes assessment that we do.

- The collaboration allows for the incorporation of more robust indicators and stated outcomes. Clarity and depth are added to our discussion of shared learning, connected learning, experiential learning, learning communities, and so on.

- As faculty and cocurricular professionals collaborate, they each redefine what it means to be student-centered as individuals and as interactive partners.

- This collaboration allows the institution to describe how it is preparing students for the realities of the 21st century (what competencies and skills are emerging). It can also provide an introspective lens to examine the impact of diversity on the undergraduate experience.

- As students begin to perceive their development as holistic learners, their motivation increases. They become more involved in regulating their own learning.

- The success of the collaboration encourages the participation of new advocates who bring varied expertise and social capital to the development of the collaboration

- The institution slowly moves away from individual audits of units, programs, divisions, departments, and so forth to an outcomes-based, information-rich model of student learning and engagement.

Community College Considerations in Student Learning Assessment

While many fundamental aspects of curricular and cocurricular assessment can be applied across two- and four-year institutions, special consideration must be given to the unique mission of community colleges and the organizational processes that support that mission.

One of the hallmarks of a comprehensive community college is the open admissions policy, which translates into the enrollment of an extremely diverse adult population. Such a policy translates into "opportunity," often multiple opportunities, for a higher education for all adults who can benefit from such an education. When one considers that students who enroll in community colleges, with or without a high school degree, represent a wide range of backgrounds, experiences, skills, abilities, and motivation, determining who can benefit before enrollment and how they benefit after enrollment is very difficult (Morante, 2002). In other words, assessment considerations that tend to be more uniform across four-year institutions must often be conceptualized differently for community colleges.

There are three areas that represent meaningful consideration for two-year institutions in conversations about assessment: college readiness and open admissions; the lack of a coordinated curricular and cocurricular experience; and the importance of access, equity, and diversity.

Many students who enroll at community colleges are woefully under prepared in terms of the basic skills of reading, writing, and mathematics; and those institutions must address the skills of these entering students. The assessment of developmental skills and courses places resource demands on the institution that cannot be delivered in other areas. While some four-year institutions also share this concern, it may not be to the same degree. Other four-year institutions do not have to engage in developmental assessment at all. For open admissions institutions assessment in developmental education is crucial because it bridges the gap between the low skill levels of many entering students and the skills needed for success in college-level courses.

Four-year and two-year institutions reflect different educational histories and philosophies. They also differ in terms of the degree to which they offer coordinated curricular and cocurricular experiences. Assessment models are much easier to implement when student populations are more homogeneous across different dimensions, experience linked courses or connected curriculums, experience intentional cocurricular experiences, share some aspect of a residential experience, and are more receptive to program review. The simple existence of an effective general education curriculum allows an institution the opportunity to examine common learning outcomes. Students at community colleges often work, have families, are first-generation college students, do not understand the culture of college, stop-out, suffer financial exigencies, and commute. Thus, assessment models at two-year institutions must account for such variables.

Two important aspects of program and institutional effectiveness that must be scrutinized relative to institutional type (four- versus two-year) are access and equity (Morante, 2002). Access refers to the percentage of the community that is served by the college and the ratio of diversity in the student population as compared to the community. In addition, the percent of students enrolled for each of several defined groups (across demographic categories) should be reasonably comparable to the population where the college is located and community served. These comparisons can be made over time to demonstrate changes both at the college level and in the community. For many two-year institutions access is a significant political consideration.

In the context of outcomes assessment, equity can refer to various things. For community colleges it can refer to the extent to which an institution or program achieves a comparable level of outcomes, direct or indirect, for various groups of enrolled students at any level. This assessment process could be carried out for any cohort of students in any area of learning and for any program, degree, service, or institution.

Access, equity and diversity represent greater assessment challenges at two-year institutions because of the greater scope of variables involved, because of temporal issues like performing longitudinal studies, and because of institutional structures that often are not capable of sustaining challenging demands.

Collaborations Can Promote 21st Century Skill Development

Many colleges and universities have committed to identifying goals and outcomes that are associated with workplace competencies and lifelong learning. More specifically, they allude to what can be called "21st century" skills and competencies that their graduates acquire(d) as part of their curricular and cocurricular experience at the institution.

If colleges and universities were pressed to provide evidence of student preparation for the realities of the 21st century, many would struggle to do so. The reasons for this are quite common. Many institutions:

- do not engage in the critical campus dialogue that would develop a consensus about these realities;

- assume that existing structures, processes, and activities (curricular and cocurricular) can promote 21st century skills and competencies;

- have never developed an assessment plan to accompany institutional efforts to prepare students for 21st century realities; and

- have not taken advantage of the rich collaborations that exist, and that could exist, between the academic and cocurricular sides to promote 21st century outcomes in students.

Twenty-first century realities in which curricular and cocurricular programs can contribute skills and competencies and that are mentioned by higher education experts, prospective employers, and career and vocational counselors are:

- global literacy;
- accelerated technology;
- social ethics and social responsibility;
- organizational networking;
- expanding diverse consumer markets;
- empowerment-oriented training and policy;
- analysis of process barriers to goal attainment;
- multicultural communities and organizations;
- understanding of teamwork in organizations;
- a fundamental understanding of the operations and assessment associated with quality and effectiveness;
- use of problem-solving in different settings and contexts; and
- development of general, specific, and contextual communication skills.

For many years cocurricular professionals have encouraged the development of student leadership that incorporated many of the aforementioned skills and competencies. Now is the time to document their presence through assessment.

Gardiner (1996) identifies the necessary conditions for these key competencies to develop in each student. Each student must have appropriate, diverse, sustained, and active student involvement in learning at every point, and be provided with both challenge and support. Development occurs gradually, through specific, deliberately designed, and consistently provided developmental experiences, across the entire curriculum and cocurriculum. This learning can be assessed using multiple methods, direct and indirect, in varying contexts. The most meaningful assessment will involve three things: clearly written outcome statements, meaningful student–student and student–faculty interactions, and frequent assessments of results coupled with timely feedback.

How might such information be used in a curricular–cocurricular collaboration to promote positive student outcomes? We know that students come to universities and colleges with a variety of self-beliefs and preparation levels, and they vary in terms of their understanding of the expectations and the reward system in higher education. Through comprehensive, systematic, and continuous assessment we can develop a profile of students that will be compared, at different points of the undergraduate experience, with the emerging profile of 21st century competencies. The resultant feedback will better inform both partners about the quality and effectiveness of their programmatic efforts.

How Designing an Assessment Effort Affects Collaborative Program Design

While it is tempting to believe that curricular and cocurricular collaborations succeed because of the presence of effective strategies and activities, the reality is that the most successful efforts use a two-pronged approach that involves (1) moving from abstract goals and objectives to something more focused and measurable and (2) using positive information and data to document the value of the program and guide program changes. The following pages are written to assist the reader in implementing this two-pronged approach to evaluate the contributions of the cocurricular experience to student learning and development.

CHAPTER 2

Overview of the Assessment Process

Assessment means various things to different people. Sometimes, its definition is dependent on the discipline background of the one approaching its implementation. For example, someone who has studied psychology has a different perspective of assessment than someone who has studied K-12 education. No one person is inaccurate. It is just that the varying definitions pose communication challenges.

For purposes of this book, we provide you with a definition of assessment. We even provide you with an operational common language for assessment and a shared conceptual understanding so that you can communicate across disciplines and across unit and program specialties. Please note that it is not so important that you use our proposed common language, definition, and conceptual understanding. It is only imperative that you decide on a definition and a common language for your unit, division, or institution, so that you can understand what each other means when you describe an objective or an outcome and thus, communicate more effectively. As important as a common language (Palomba & Banta, 1999; Upcraft & Schuh, 1996) and agreed-upon assessment definition, is the consistency in philosophy of why you are engaging in assessment. A shared conceptual understanding of assessment (Maki, 2001) allows individuals the opportunity to remind each other about why you are engaging in assessment and what you hope to gain from it.

Definition of Assessment and Shared Conceptual Understanding

As we mentioned, there are various definitions of assessment. Often, the definition of assessment and the shared conceptual understanding of assessment are found in the motivation for doing assessment (Maki,

2001). In other words, if you want to engage in assessment in order to improve your programs, you will see the desire to improve embedded in how you practice assessment and those reasons will be weaved into shared campus conversations. If you are occupied with assessment in order to meet accreditation standards only, then your shared conversations and implementation of assessment practice may be very compliant driven (Palomba & Banta, 1999). If you are conducting assessment because you feel you have to defend your programs, than your conceptual understanding may lie in a need to have vigorous research standards embedded into your assessment, thus allowing you to "prove" your program's worth to any and all constituents (Upcraft & Schuh, 1996).

Marchese (1998) states "assessment is the systematic collection, review, and use of information about educational programs undertaken for the purpose of improving student learning and development" (p. 4). Mentkowski (1998) explains, "assessment is a set of processes designed to improve, demonstrate, and inquire about student learning" (p. 1).

Palomba and Banta (1999) write that the "the overriding purpose of assessment is to understand how educational programs are working and to determine whether they are contributing to student growth and development" (p. 20). Huba and Freed (2000) define assessment as "the process of gathering and discussing information from multiple and diverse sources in order to develop a deep understanding of what students know, understand, and can do with their knowledge as a result of their educational experiences; the process culminates when assessment results are used to improve subsequent learning." (p. 8) You can see through these definitions that the shared thread is the emphasis on gathering information about a particular program or a group of programs in order to improve that program or programs—all the while contributing to student development and learning.

Adapted from North Carolina State University's *Committee on Undergraduate Program Review (CUPR) Guidelines* (2001a), assessment is putting into place a systematic process that will answer the following questions on a continuous, ongoing basis:

- What are we trying to do and why?
- What is my program supposed to accomplish?
- How well are we doing it?
- How do we know?
- How do we use the information to improve or celebrate successes?
- Do the improvements we make work? (Bresciani, 2002, p. 1)

Given this operational definition, which is the one we will use throughout this book, assessment moves from the unattainable, rigorous research-driven model to one that is embedded in the day-to-day of our doing. You can see by the questions posed that assessment requires practitioners to reflect on what they believe they are accomplishing. It causes them to ask why a program exists and what it is to achieve (Table 2–1). Also embedded in this latter definition is a shared conceptual understanding of assessment. Assessment is viewed here as a means to improve a program, as well as to improve student learning and development (Palomba & Banta, 1999). The perception that assessment is about better understanding how we deliver certain end results means that assessment is not viewed as assessment "for assessment's sake." Thus, assessment is a systematic process by which services and student learning are improved (Banta, Black, & Kline, 2001).

A Common Language

In establishing a common language for your unit, division, or institutional assessment plan, it may be helpful to first think of it in the context of the definition of assessment (Palomba & Banta, 1999). If we diagram the assessment cycle questions (Table 2–2), it would look something like the following diagram (Figure 2–1), the text version of which can be used to construct a plan for implementing assessment (Bresciani, 2002, p.1).

TABLE 2–1

First Things First
(Source: Bresciani, 2003a.)

- Acknowledge why you are engaging in outcomes assessment.
- Define assessment and your shared conceptual understanding of assessment.
- Define a common language.
- Acknowledge your political environment.
- Identify your role in the evaluation.
- Articulate your assessment expectation(s).
- Identify what you have already done concerning evaluation, assessment, and planning.
- Identify easy-to-access resources (e.g., data, assessment tools, people, technology).
- Establish a support system.
- Just dive in—assessment is an iterative process.

The "What are we trying to do and why?" piece is equal to the articulation of the mission or purpose, and the program's objectives or goals. "What is my program supposed to accomplish?" are the outcomes. "How well are we doing it?" includes the methods for gathering the evidence as well as the planning and operation involved in implementing the outcomes. "How do we know?" incorporates the gathering of evidence and the interpretation of that evidence. "How do we use the information to improve or celebrate successes?" involves making decisions and recommendations based on the interpretation of the findings. Finally, "Do the improvements

TABLE 2–2

Assessment Cycle Questions
(Source: Bresciani, 2002, p.1.)

- What are we trying to do and why?
- What is my program supposed to accomplish?
- How well are we doing it?
- How do we know?
- How do we use the information to improve or celebrate successes?
- Do the improvements we make work?

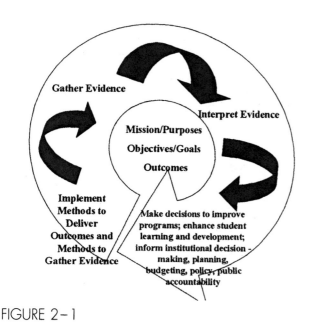

Gather Evidence

Interpret Evidence

Mission/Purposes
Objectives/Goals
Outcomes

Implement
Methods to
Deliver
Outcomes and
Methods to
Gather Evidence

Make decisions to improve
programs; enhance student
learning and development;
inform institutional decision -
making, planning,
budgeting, policy, public
accountability

FIGURE 2–1

The Iterative Assessment Cycle
(Sources: Adapted from Maki, 2001 and Bresciani, 2003a.)

we make work?" includes following up on the changes that were made, maybe one semester later, maybe two to four years later, in order to make sure that the stated changes worked.

Note that one of the most prominent words in describing the following diagram is the word *iterative* (Maki, 2001). Conducting assessment is not like writing a thesis or dissertation. While it may feel like it at times, the purpose, as we mentioned, is to find out how well your program is working so that you can make improvements to your program. The word *iterative*, literally means "involving repetition: as **a** : expressing repetition of a verbal action **b** : relating to or being iteration of an operation or procedure" (http://www.m-w.com/ cgi-bin/dictionary). Iterative describes the nature of engaging in the assessment process. For example, from assessment you may learn that you did not implement your program to meet a particular outcome and then you will find yourself either changing the stated outcome or changing how you implement your program. You may learn that a particular assessment method did not evaluate a stated outcome, so the following year or semester you need to plan a different way to capture the evidence of the learning or development. You will discover unintended outcomes. These are outcomes you did not set out to measure, and they may be outcomes you had no idea were a part of your program. Sometimes they are positive; sometimes they are not.

Iterative is a very important word and a very important practice to remember when engaging in assessment.

Before continuing with the diagram explanation, it would be best to provide some definitions—a common language—for we may have already used terms that you define differently. Again, the purpose of defining a common language is not so that you adopt what is proposed in this book. Instead, the purpose is to illustrate the need of defining these terms on your own campus, so that you understand each other across units, programs, and disciplines. As we explore the common language, you may find the following outline helpful for drafting assessment plans and for 'closing the loop' (Maki, 2001) of the assessment cycle (e.g., making decisions based on your assessment findings).

Program
The program is that which delivers the end results of what you are assessing. It is anything that has an autonomous set of outcomes. (This will make more sense after reading about outcomes.) So for now, you can choose your set of responsibilities and call it a program, or your set of responsibilities may separate into multiple programs. Or your set of responsibilities may be classified as a set of activities within a program. Again, it will become clearer how to organize once you begin to articulate outcomes and assessment measures.

Mission or Purpose
The mission or purpose of your program may be the same thing. Since this is not a book about strategic planning, we will not get into a lot of detail about how to write an effective mission. Suffice it to say that your mission is to illustrate the purpose of your program (Sybouts, 1992). The point of including it in an assessment plan is to provide you with a framework from which to proceed in the crafting of objectives and outcomes (Nichols, 1995). If you do not have an official mission statement, do not worry. You can still engage in outcomes assessment. Some programs have formulated their mission statement from their outcomes.

Goals and Objectives
For the purpose of this book, goals and objectives mean the same thing. After we explain the meaning, we will be referring to these only as objectives. Goals and objectives generally describe what the program intends to accomplish (Maki, 2001). Through goals and objectives, the program's mission comes to life in that objectives

further explain the purpose of the program. Goals and objectives often articulate the values of the program, allowing for further description and meaning to be communicated to all constituents (Nichols, 1995).

According to NC State's *CUPR Common Language* (2001b), objectives (a.k.a. "goals") are defined as "broad, general statements of [1] what the program wants students to be able to do and to know or [2] what the program will do to ensure what students will be able to do and to know. Objectives are evaluated directly or indirectly by measuring specific outcomes related to the objective. Program objectives are related to the mission and objectives of the department and college in which the program resides, and to the mission and objectives of the University" (p. 1). This is the definition we will be using in this book.

Following are questions to ask after writing your objectives that may prove beneficial to your assessment planning and reflection of your program (Bresciani, 2003b, p.1):

- Is it meaningful? In other words, does this objective have meaning to program planners and the students who are involved in the program? Does the objective mean something to internal and external constituents of the program?

- Is it important? Similar to "meaningful," is the objective important to program planners and the students who are involved in the program? Does the objective have significance to internal and external constituents of the program?

- Is it a broad, general statement of either what the program wants students to be able to do and to know, or what the program will do to ensure what students will be able to do and to know?

- Is it related to my department or program mission and objectives?

- Is there an accompanying outcome to measure this objective?

Outcomes

Outcomes specifically describe the end result of the program. They express what students, administrators, faculty, and staff should know or do. These outcomes must be measurable. However, when we say "measurable," we do not want you to think that they must necessarily be "countable." What we mean by measurable is that you must be able to identify or observe how you

know the students are able to do what you said they would be able to do as a result of your program or combination of programs. In addition, you must be able to gather evidence that learning or development occurred. Furthermore,

> Outcomes are more detailed and specific statements derived from the objectives. Outcomes are specifically about what you want the end result of your efforts to be. It is not what you are going to do to the student, but rather what you want the student to know or do as a result of an initiative, course, or activity. In order to be measurable (e.g., identifiable vs. countable), outcomes typically use active verbs such as demonstrate, articulate, illustrate, conduct, define, describe, apply, compose, integrate, convince, create, plan, compare, and summarize. (Bresciani, 2003b, p.1)

When writing outcomes, it may be helpful to incorporate appropriate program standards, such as those espoused by the Council for the Advancement of Standards in Higher Education (CAS), where applicable. It may be useful to incorporate appropriate accreditation standards as well. In addition, it may be valuable for planning purposes to divide the outcomes into categories (Bresciani, 2003b; Hanson & Bresciani, 2003; Maki, 2001; Palomba & Banta, 1999; Upcraft & Schuh,1996). For example:

- Program outcomes illustrate what you want your program to accomplish.

- Student learning and development outcomes depict cognitive abilities, as well as affective dimensions that you desire your program to instill or enhance.

- Input outcomes typically define your standards for student acceptance and participation into particular programs.

- Student needs outcomes are where students prioritize their service and educational needs. The students' learned articulation of needs often informs the writing of program outcomes.

- Service utilization outcomes seek to set standards for the utilization of services and facilities.

This book primarily focuses on the assessment of student learning and development outcomes. Thus, understanding the difference between student learning and development outcomes from some of these other outcomes will be the focus of the next chapter.

Following are questions that may help you reflect on your program and know whether you have written a meaningful and manageable outcome:

- Is it measurable? Again, this question seeks to focus not on whether you can count the result of the outcome, but on whether you can identify or observe when you know the outcome has been met. So, if it helps, you may want to insert another question here such as, Is this outcome identifiable or observable?

- Is it meaningful? In other words, does the outcome have meaning to program planners and the students who are involved in the program? Does the outcome mean something to internal and external constituents of the program? Is the outcome addressing a "hot issue" or an espoused value?

- Is it manageable? This is a key question. The outcome has to be manageable in that it has to be incorporated into the day-to-day business of the program. This is not to say that every outcome articulated by a program has to be measured every year. On the contrary, spreading the assessment of outcomes over a logical three-to five-year cycle makes for the inclusion of the process into the day-to-day business possible. For example, one year you may need to plan to assess whether or not you meet certain program standards such as CAS, the next year you may want to focus on evaluating substandard areas to see how to improve them, and the following year you may want to evaluate how you are contributing to learning principles espoused by your institution's general education plan. What you are trying to do here is create "habits" of assessment. Take one step at a time. Ask yourself if you can fit the assessment of this outcome into your day-to-day business, or whether you need to plan a rigorous research project to accomplish that which you desire to know. If you need to conduct the rigorous research first, then you may need to think about how meaningful it is to have that portion in your assessment plan prior to conducting the evaluation needed to answer your questions

about your program's performance. For example, if you desire to know whether students are learning leadership development skills from your leadership workshop series, it may be that you can incorporate evaluation tools right into the series—making it a part of your day-to-day planning and implementing of services. Or it may be that you first need to conduct a cohort analysis to identify all the areas of the where and what students are learning about leadership during their academic career in order to recast your leadership series to better influence intended outcomes.

- Who will I be gathering evidence from to know that my outcome has been met? This question is to provide the planner with some information to understand whether the students for whom the outcomes are intended are the only source of whether the outcome has been met. Consider the example that you would like to know if your student government leaders are meeting your intended outcome of "able to identify student issues and compare and contrast opposing arguments for solutions to those issues." The student government leaders' ability to demonstrate this is one logical point in which to gather evidence. The other place may be the administrators and faculty leaders with whom these students interact to collect opposing opinions. Perhaps even the student newspaper reporters will be able to comment on how informed the student leaders are on opposing views of their given agenda(s). Identifying these other constituents of the outcome means that you may want to gather evidence from them as to the extent to which they believe the outcome has been met.

- Who would know if my outcome has been met? The purpose of this question is to help the planner identify people who can assist with articulating how anyone would know whether the outcome has been met. Similar to the example posed in the previous question, faculty and administrators working with the student government leaders may have a different idea about what it means for a student leader to be "able to identify student issues and compare and contrast opposing arguments for solutions to those issues." Having those conversations with the constituents will not only help them understand what you are attempting to accomplish through your program, but also enable them to see the direct educational value of your program come alive as they begin to partner with you to articulate what this all means and what it all looks like. In addition, conversations of students' varying cognitive and psychosocial abilities begin to help transform expectations and understanding of students' performances.

- How will I know if it has been met? Similar to the preceding explanation for each question, this is posed to assist the planner to think about the meaningfulness of the outcome, whether it is measurable, and how the assessment planner will know that it is measurable. In other words, what does meeting this outcome look like? How do you know the intended learning or development has occurred? Many times, practitioners will "freeze" when we ask them this question. All we really want to know is, How did you identify that particular desired learning or behavior in the past? After that question is posed, we usually see faces light up, and then there is an answer. As practitioners, we typically do know "it" when we see "it;" we have just never had to articulate what we were looking for before.

- Will it provide me with evidence that will lead me to make a decision for continuous improvement (Deming, 1986)? This is another key question. As we mentioned, our definition of assessment requires the reflection of evaluating the program with the assumption that you are gathering information that will help you improve your program. And thus, outcomes such as "will deliver twenty-four educational programs in the residence halls" do not tell you anything about how to improve your educational programs in the residence halls. You may need to articulate the aforementioned outcome for program reasons (and that is no problem) in order to understand how to improve your educational programs. However, you will need to begin to also illustrate particular end results of what you wanted those education programs to accomplish, such as "students can translate reasons for hall safety rules into consequences for breaking hall safety rules." (Bresciani, 2003b)

Drafting meaningful and measurable outcomes is a time-consuming process. For more detailed assistance

in drafting outcomes, refer to the books *Assessment Essentials* (Palomba & Banta, 1999) or *Writing Measurable and Meaningful Outcomes* (Bresciani, 2001). Do not be discouraged if it takes a considerable amount of time for you to draft outcomes for which your entire staff is pleased. Writing measurable and meaningful outcomes is typically not an overnight assignment. It may take a while, but do not wait until they are perfect before trying to assess them. When you begin to assess your outcomes, you may just discover that you have articulated better outcomes than you thought. If not, all you have to do is refine them until they are more meaningful and manageable.

Student Behavior as an Outcome

Because many cocurricular specialists believe that the culmination of the learning is changed behavior, we often get questions on the assessment of students' behavior. While it may be true that many of you have the positions you do because you care about how students behave, and the ability to change behavior may be the ultimate end result of learning- and development-focused programs, attempting to evaluate behavior or to have your program's success measured as a result of students' behavior is something we do not encourage. Should you choose to have your program's success defined by your ability to change students' behavior and not to demonstrate the extent to which they know how to change their own behavior, then we highly recommend that you separate the behavior-changing outcomes from those outcomes that articulate learning and development. In other words, if you want to keep outcomes that illustrate behavior change, also include outcomes that demonstrate that you taught the students how to change their behavior. Thus, you can demonstrate that even though students' behaviors did not change, your program still taught them how to behave in the appropriate manner.

For example, rather than just stating *students will make ethical decisions*, you may want to assess the extent to which students define and describe ethical behavior. Then you may want to examine the extent to which students apply and analyze ethical behavior or the lack thereof in case studies. The next considerations may be whether students can compose an ethical dilemma case study for a situation within which they find themselves; and, finally, whether they can discriminate between ethical and unethical behavior in a case study presented to them by one of their peers. In this manner, you are assessing the degree to which the students can apply what you have taught them, but you are not taking responsibility for their decisions to use and apply that knowledge in real life.

If you noted the use of *Bloom's Taxonomy* (University of Victoria, 1956) in the aforementioned example, you are not mistaken. "Benjamin Bloom created this taxonomy for categorizing levels of abstraction of questions that commonly occur in educational settings" (retrieved from http://www.coun.uvic.ca/learn/program/hnd-outs/bloom.html). This taxonomy is a wonderful resource to use when drafting student learning and development outcomes. When using *Taxonomy* to write outcomes, students' abilities to demonstrate competencies in the stated manner allow you to take control of what you are able to do in your program, while leaving the decisions made with that knowledge up to the students themselves.

Evaluation Methods

Since evaluation methods are a major portion of this book, we will explore several methods in the chapters dedicated to assessment methods and tools. Be sure to read Chapter Four, "Introduction to Assessment Tools," prior to reading about any of the assessment methods so that you can ensure meaningful interpretation and application of the proposed tools.

Implementation of Assessment

The implementation of assessment is all about the details of who is doing what when. Here is where making the assessment plan (e.g., the planning to answer all the previously posed questions) manageable and incorporating it into day-to-day activities comes alive. Here is where the planner illustrates when outcomes would be written and later refined, when assessment methods and tools would be selected and either purchased or developed, when tools would be administered, and when analysis of data and interpretation occur. In addition, plans for documenting and disseminating results and making decisions based on those results are also specified. Why this much detail? Without it, sophisticated plans easily become unmanageable or simple plans are never implemented, all because the time for implementation was never factored into the day-to-day activities of delivering the actual program that is being assessed.

In addition, the implementation plan helps your external constituents see when you will be assessing the outcome that is so valuable to them and that you cannot reasonably measure all your outcomes in one year. Having a documented multiyear assessment plan has, on many occasions, helped us have the conversation with our constituents about priorities and that if one outcome needs to be assessed now, then another must be deferred to a later time. This planning also allows you to identify the resources you will need to carry out your assessment plan and thus enable you to make any refinements based on research skill or resource limitations. In addition, the assessment plan helps demonstrate whether you are committed to ongoing (e.g., annual) systematic (e.g., planned) assessment. An example of a multiyear assessment plan can be found at http://www.ncsu.edu/undergrad_affairs/assessment/files/projects/stu_con_plan_0204.pdf.

Finally, in the implementation of the assessment plan is where you plan for the actual implementation of programs, workshops, and training sessions designed to deliver as well as measure the intended outcomes. This is the portion of the assessment plan where you may identify that which you have learned does not already exist in your program and should. In other words, recognizing that you want students to be able to apply conflict resolutions skills to specific situations, but realizing you have never provided the students with an opportunity to understand when the application of conflict resolution skills is called for and when it is not. Thus, you may first need to plan for the actual delivery of the information to students before you can evaluate whether the students have learned.

Results, Decisions, and Recommendations

While you most likely have learned how to report results of your research projects, presenting results of assessment findings may be very much the same or it may be very different, depending on the research rigor of your assessment cycle. In any event, reporting results in a meaningful way and with a strategic timeline and plan is essential in order for the assessment to have a positive effect on improvement. In other words, you may not want to just write your results and then take them to a committee for decisions of continuous improvement to be made. You may want to strategically release your results to certain individuals or committees in order to work on solutions and action plans (e.g., decisions and recommendations), and then share both the results and decisions and recommendations with other constituents, inviting additional feedback for the improvement of your program (Hanson & Bresciani, 2003; Palomba & Banta, 1999; Upcraft & Schuh, 1996).

Writing meaningful results so that they can be understood and applied to decisions and recommendations is essential to effective assessment (Hanson, 2003). While some of the chapters in this book offer suggestions for writing results based on the tools that you may choose to use, the following suggestions from Ewell (1994), Hanson and Bresciani (2003), Palomba and Banta (1999), and Upcraft and Schuh (1996) are presented in order to serve as reminders of how to report your results and decisions effectively:

- Identify the values of your constituents and find out how your constituents prefer to see data and reports. Oftentimes you will need to revise your presentation for each group of your constituents. In other words, you will have different presentations for your bosses, students, office staff, trustees, and parents. In many cases, these types of constituents have varying values and the data you present to them must reflect their values as well as be presented in a manner that resonates with them. For example, it may be typical that trustees prefer to see charts and graphs that very quickly, in one glance, tell them the story of your assessment findings. Students, on the other hand, may prefer to see more details about the findings and the posed potential solutions.

- Students can be extremely helpful, not only in collecting the assessment information but also in your writing and dissemination of results and decisions made. They can often advise the strategic delivery route of the data so that you can garner the students' interest and expertise in order to make the change occur. Another positive outcome of inviting student assistance is that students can help spread the word that something is being done with all that data that they helped collect.

- Be sure to link the data and decisions made to the outcome and the program being assessed (Maki, 2001). This emphasizes accountability and moves your organization toward values expressed by a learning community.

- Timing is everything when delivering results and decisions. Pay attention to the political climate on your campus, and respect the proper reporting channels. While it is not typically a good idea to

delay sharing what you have learned from your assessment process, sometimes the environment is such that the sharing of particular information will not be noticed or well received, regardless of its positive outcomes.

- Prepare to defend your outcome, evaluation method, results, and the decisions made based on those results. There is always someone who will identify something wrong with what you have learned. That is just the way it is. Similar to the stories you have heard about thesis or dissertation defense, just have an answer—a reason for making the decisions that you did, whether it be in regards to the crafting of the outcome, the selection of the assessment method, the type of analysis run, or the interpretation of the data. And if you do not have a reason or an answer, do not make one up. Systematic assessment can be undermined very quickly if the integrity of the practice is in question.

- To the best of your ability, stick with your assessment plan schedule for analyzing, interpreting, and writing the results of your assessment plan (Table 2–3). We can attest to the fact that life interferes with work and work interferes with assessment. However, the longer you wait to interpret assessment results and document the decisions that need to be made, the less likely you will do so. It is just too hard to get back to the data, recall why and when you did what, and find the information you need to inform your decisions. At times, we have taken three times as long as we should have to write the results and decisions made after having abandoned the "closing the loop" portion of the assessment process. It is a painful process that we wish for you to avoid.

- If you need help interpreting the data, get it. Your assessment team may be of help or you may ask one of your faculty colleagues or another cocurricular specialist. If you are fearful of anyone seeing the data prior to your understanding it, then it may be worth it for you to invest in a consultant.

- Release every assessment report in draft form until you have visited with everyone that you know you need to have visited with in order to make the decision or recommendation you need to make. At the point that you feel you have

15

saturated conversation on the topic, you can remove the draft from the assessment report and publish it to your website.

Finally, remember that thinking your data told you absolutely nothing about your outcomes is not necessarily an accurate interpretation. We have learned a great deal about our assessment methods, tools, and outcomes from "failed" assessment cycles. We have been able to make several decisions when it seemed that the data showed us nothing. In fact when the data did not seem to say anything, we often learned that we could not have met a particular outcome because we had nothing in our program that was intended to deliver that outcome. Or we learned that a particular outcome was not feasible until we had more program facilitators agreeing to implement the outcome and agreeing on what meeting the outcome looked like. All the decisions that have arisen from "failed" assessment plans have still enabled us to improve programs and reassess more effectively in the following year.

TABLE 2–3

Typical Components of An Assessment Plan
(Source: Bresciani, 2003b.)

- Mission
- Objectives
- Outcomes
- Evaluation methods

By outcomes with criteria
- Implementation of assessment

Who is Responsible for What – When?
- Results
- Decisions and recommendations

Purpose of Assessment

It may seem a little odd to be almost completely through the assessment overview chapter and then to have an explanation on the purpose of assessment. We thought that you would not have picked up this book had you not seen some value in doing assessment. However, just in case you are not convinced, we propose the following reasons for doing assessment and, thus, the uses of assessment. The following list has been

compiled based on the research of the American Association for Higher Education (1994), Bresciani (2003a), Ewell (1997a), Maki (2001), Palomba and Banta (1999), and Upcraft and Schuh (1996).

Assessment can fulfill the following purposes:

- <u>Reinforce or emphasize the mission of your unit.</u> As you discovered from reading through the design of an assessment plan, engaging in assessment planning causes one to reflect upon the mission and purpose of your program and thus how it relates to the unit's mission under which you are housed, your division's mission, and your institutional mission. You do not necessarily have to panic if you do not see your program's outcomes and values reflected in your unit's or division's mission, however it will help you to be aware of this as you enter into policy and resource allocation discussions.

- <u>Improve a program's quality or performance.</u> Palomba and Banta (1999) call this formative assessment in that evaluation "is meant to 'form' the program or performance" (p. 7). In other words, you evaluate the program while you are delivering it so you can tweak it as you go. This helps you meet your intended outcomes for the entire program, because you are assessing progress towards those outcomes along the way.

- <u>Compare a program's quality or value to the program's previously defined principles.</u> Palomba and Banta (1999) define this as summative assessment meaning "to make judgments about" (p. 7). Here, you are evaluating whether your program has met its outcomes once you have completed a program offering.

- <u>Inform planning.</u> As you realize, effective systematic assessment cannot be carried out without good planning. And when it is carried out, it can inform the planning of future programs, as practitioners now understand what works well and why and what is not working so well.

- <u>Inform decision-making.</u> Decision-making is key to any genuine assessment process.

- <u>Inform policy discussions at the local, state, regional, and national levels.</u> Effective assessment can identify where there is need for policies to be formulated in order for improvements to be made. We often get questions about whether people should make recommendations to another program or policy-forming body when they have discovered that a program not under their supervision, or a policy or lack of a policy is believed to be having an adverse effect on their program outcomes. Our answer is a resounding *yes* if your political environment allows for such sharing. The evidence you collect can help inform the types of policy discussions on which your program is depending.

- Evaluate programs and personnel (should you choose to include personnel evaluation). We caution the use of program assessment to evaluate personnel prior to your having established a culture in which results are used to make decisions to improve programs. Using assessment results to sanction personnel will most likely create a culture where program administrators are fearful of uncovering their needed improvements and thus do not engage in meaningful assessment.

- Assist in the request for additional funds from the college or university and external community. While we often get the question of which assessment methods will be most effective in securing internal and external resources, our answer is dependent upon the outcome you are assessing, the methods and tools you are using to assess the outcome, and the type of data and reporting format that will have more meaning to the constituents you are trying to influence. However, note that no matter how thorough you are, no matter how rigorous your assessment plan and research methods are, someone will always find fault in your work. The best piece of advice we have ever heard, but have not yet had the nerve to use, was stated by Gary Hanson of Arizona State University (Hanson & Bresciani, 2003). Dr. Hanson advises that when your constituents are tearing apart your assessment methods, conclusions, decisions, and recommendations, ask a simple question, "What evidence did you use to make this decision last year?" It stumps them every time, he says, and we believe this would be true for most practitioners needing to pose this question.

- Assist in the reallocation of resources. Remember that while everything in the aforementioned bullet applies here, internal reallocation also includes time, expertise, staff assignments, and sharing of resources across unit and division lines.

- Assist in meeting accreditation requirements, models of best practices, and national benchmarks. As you may be aware, regional higher education accrediting bodies are demanding more genuine engagement in outcomes assessment, and we are delighted to see this. For some of you, this reality may have caused you to buy this book and to begin thinking about how to implement outcomes assessment in your program. For others, you have been waiting a long time for accreditors to value the experts' (e.g., you, the practitioner's) ability to define what is of value to their programs (e.g., outcomes) and find practical and meaningful ways to gather information to improve.

- Celebrate successes. This is one purpose we often forget about and one that is worth paying attention to, as we have suffered in the past from not having enough evidence to celebrate our successes. It is in celebrating the successes of what our programs accomplish, as evidenced by assessment, that we are able to more meaningfully engage in assessment.

- Reflect on the attitudes and approaches we take in improving learning and development. This purpose cannot be highlighted enough. We have seen programs improve when they were in the first steps of identifying their outcomes. When program professionals come together to discuss with each other what they understand they are trying to accomplish, veterans have an opportunity to educate new professionals, and new professionals energize veterans with innovative solutions and approaches. Often, delivery of services is improved because the services are distributed more purposefully, and thus the outcomes are understood not only by the cocurricular specialists delivering them but also by the students who are benefactors of the services. In attempt to answer the simple question of why are we doing this, or why we are doing it this way, time is often reallocated into making processes more efficient and effective.

- <u>Create a culture of continuous improvement—a culture of accountability, learning, and improvement.</u> This purpose is what we believe assessment is all about. Again, you may ascribe to another definition of assessment, and that is just fine. But in order for this book to make any sense to you, it is important to remember that everything we are discussing is couched in this purpose. Assessment is not for the sake of assessment. Rather, through assessment, one can create a culture of continuous improvement—a culture of accountability, learning, and improvement (Maki, 2001).

TABLE 2-4

The Most Important Qualities of Assessment
(Source: Bresciani, 2003a.)

- Meaningful in that it is faculty- and cocurricular specialist- or expert-driven
- Manageable in that it considers varying resources
- Flexible in that it factors in assessment learning curves
- Truth-seeking, objective, and ethical
- Informs decisions for continuous improvement or provides evidence of proof
- Promotes a culture of accountability, learning, and improvement

18

CHAPTER 3

Moving from Assessing Satisfaction to Assessing Student Learning and Development

Why Move Away from Student Satisfaction Assessment?

The assessment of student satisfaction, needs, and service utilization is very important. It has great purpose, particularly for constituents who place a heavy emphasis on students' approval ratings. However, findings from this type of assessment do not necessarily help you understand your program's contributions to the greater work of the university. In other words, the assessment findings do not tell you how your program contributes to student development and learning, and the findings seldom help you make decisions for continuous improvement of your programs.

The argument for assessing student learning and development in order to gain better information to make decisions for continuous improvement can best be illustrated by example. The following example, from Career Services, was adapted from an article in the National Association of Student Personnel Administrator's (NASPA's) *NetResults*, entitled "Outcomes Assessment in Student Affairs: Moving Beyond Satisfaction to Student Learning and Development" (Bresciani, 2002).

> The sample satisfaction outcome is "97% of the career service participants will agree or strongly agree that career service programs provided information and assistance that were helpful to their preparation to leave the University." While this appears to be a well-written outcome, there are questions we have for the outcome writer. In addition to the questions posed in chapter two (Is it measurable? Is it meaningful? Is it manageable? Who will I be gathering evidence from to know

that my outcome has been met? Who would know if my outcome has been met? How will I know if it has been met? Will it provide me with evidence that will lead me to make a decision for continuous improvement?), we pose the following.

1) Why 97%? What does 97% represent? Note that by asking this question, we are not looking for a right or wrong answer. We just want to understand if 97% has some meaning for those engaging in the assessment of this program? After all, if outcomes are going to be used to inform decisions for continuous improvement, the decision-makers need to understand if 97% holds some particular meaning. Again, in posing this question, we are not looking for a particular answer, we are only seeking a meaningful reason.

2) What information and assistance were helpful? In other words if 97% of the students agree and strongly agree to this statement, what services did they find helpful? Likewise, if 97% disagree, what services are they not finding helpful?

Note once more that this was a well-written outcome and it serves a purpose. Through the articulation of this outcome and the gathering of responses, this administrator now can illustrate the helpfulness of his/her offices' services. However, if the administrator has missed the 97% mark, how does he/she know what to improve?

To further illustrate, consider how this outcome would be assessed. A locally developed self-report survey could be administered. Career Service specialists may even observe student satisfaction or interview students individually or in focus groups to gather satisfaction information. With that in mind, ask the questions posed in chapter four (What is my budget? What is my timeline? What are my analysis capabilities? Who needs to see this data? How easily can I fit this method into my annual responsibilities? Who needs to make decisions with this data? Will this kind of evidence help me make the decisions I need to make? How will I document the evidence and the decisions made from that evidence?). [Consult Table 3–1 as well.]

TABLE 3–1

Questions to Ask Yourself
(Source: Bresciani, 2002.)

1. Will this assessment method help me understand what it is that I am doing that is contributing to the end result stated in this outcome?

2. Will this assessment method help me understand why I am delivering the services in the way that I am?

3. Will the evidence collected from this method help me make the decisions I need to improve my program or help me understand how to maintain status quo?

We may be able to figure out how these questions are answered by data that would be gathered to measure whether "97% of the career service participants will agree or strongly agree that career service programs provided information and assistance that were helpful to their preparation to leave the University."

However, if you only use a self-report satisfaction survey, that type of data could not answer the aforementioned questions. Again, this is not a discussion about the importance of student satisfaction outcomes. It is of great value to know whether your students are satisfied with your services; however, this type of information does not typically tell you if your program is accomplishing what it is meant to accomplish. It also usually does not inform you about how you may be contributing to student development and learning.

Other Reasons for Assessing Student Learning and Development

Chapter One described several reasons to consider the assessment of student learning and development. If you skipped the first chapter, we offer four quotes to help you understand the purpose of assessing student learning and development.

1) "The concepts of 'learning', 'personal development', and 'student development' are inextricably intertwined and inseparable" (Schroeder, Blimling, McEwen, & Schuh, 1996, p. 118). Scholars from the field are calling for student and academic support services professionals to assess what they do. As previously mentioned, it is often quite controversial for cocurricular specialists to enter the student learning conversation, thus, we are not differentiating between the assessment of affective and cognitive outcomes. As such, we are trying to avoid academic arguments over the delineation between affective and cognitive abilities in an effort to focus higher education professionals on better understanding their contributions to student learning.

2) The National Research Council (2001) reports that "advances in the study of thinking and learning (cognitive science) and in the field of measurement have stimulated people to think in new ways about how students learn and what they know, what is therefore worth assessing, and how to obtain useful information about student competencies." (p. 16). Nationally, attention has turned to understanding how student learning is delivered. Many are being asked to illustrate how their services contribute to student learning.

3) "To assure that students have sufficient and various kinds of educational opportunities to learn or develop desired outcomes, faculty and staff often engage in curricular and cocurricular mapping" (Maki, 2001). Maki has articulated the importance of tying academic courses and cocurricular activities to program outcomes. Maki's vision is for everyone involved in any aspect of higher education to be able to diagram or map how their program activities contribute to institutional student learning principles or institutional competencies. In mapping these outcomes, cocurricular specialists can engage in the ever-important

institutional conversations about student learning principles and values.

4) "The institution provides student support programs, services, and activities consistent with its mission that promote student learning and enhance the development of its students" (Southern Association of Colleges and Schools, 2000) While this is a quote from only one regional institutional accreditor, many regional institutional accreditation organizations have begun to place more emphasis on the assessment of student learning. In so doing, regional accreditors have placed the expectation upon all those involved with students to articulate their contributions to student learning and to assess that contribution.

Expectations have been set for all to articulate their contributions to student learning. We know that student affairs and academic support service professionals are partners in learning and development. Thus as educators, these cocurricular specialists are expected to assess the development and learning outcomes of their programs.

The Transition Process from Assessing Satisfaction to Assessing Student Learning and Development

As we talk to people about moving away from assessing student satisfaction to assessing student learning, we remind them that it takes time. It is truly an evolution (Maki, 2001). If you have not ever successfully assessed student satisfaction, then it may not be the best use of your time to immediately begin to assess student learning and development. As we discussed earlier, engaging in systematic, meaningful assessment means that, similar to establishing other good practices, you have to begin to develop habits—habits of assessment.

Think of the analogy of trying to get in shape. When you are training for a 10 K run, you do not just jump into your racquetball shoes and run 20 K. You start small by researching and purchasing the proper training gear, taking time to stretch, running short distances, paying attention to your knee pain, and drinking plenty of fluids. The same is true for assessing student learning and development. Most cocurricular professionals do not just decide one day to assess student learning. They build up to it. They typically try to successfully assess student satisfaction first and then move, over time, to assessing student learning. This is not to infer, however,

that you have to start with assessing satisfaction before you can assess student learning.

To illustrate, return to our earlier example outcome: "97% of the career service participants will agree or strongly agree that career service programs provided information and assistance that were helpful to their preparation to leave the University." Let's examine the steps that one would take to move it from satisfaction into student learning and development.

The first step would be breaking the outcome down into the desired end results of what information and assistance is offered that would be helpful to students' preparation to leave the university. In order to do this, we return to the iterative assessment cycle and ask the following questions:

- What do students need to know in order to be well prepared to leave the institution?

- How are we teaching them that information?

- Do we provide them opportunities prior to their leaving for them to demonstrate that they have learned what we think they should?

- How will we know that they have learned what we think they should?

Before using the answers to these questions to re-craft the outcomes, note that the transformation has begun for many professionals by merely discussing the answers to these questions among their staff (Maki, 2003). While many may have already had these conversations, some have not and thus find themselves moving away from discussions about making sure we provide "x" and "y" to a commitment to understanding whether our students have learned "x" and "y" and how we know. What is the difference? The difference is that the conversation and resulting practice moves from comments such as, "we have to offer this activity regardless of whether students are attending and learning" to asking the question of "how best will students learn what we need them to learn in order for them to be prepared?"

For those of you who have already had these exchanges, it becomes a matter of articulating that which you desire the student to be able to know and do as a result of participating in your services. Examine the following reworked outcomes:

- Students will demonstrate appropriate interview skills during videotaped mock interviews.

- Students will articulate a high level of confidence in their career choice.
- Students will analyze the job market and identify at least three types of fields for which they are qualified. Students will document their qualifications for at least three types of positions in their resume and performance portfolios.

In looking at the outcomes, ask the questions from Chapter Two: Is it measurable? Is it meaningful? Is it manageable? Who will I be gathering evidence from to know that my outcome has been met? Who would know if my outcome has been met? How will I know if it has been met? Will it provide me with evidence that will lead me to make a decision for continuous improvement? Just a reminder, do not be discouraged if it takes a while for you to draft outcomes for which the entire staff is pleased. As mentioned in Chapter Two, writing measurable and meaningful outcomes is typically not an overnight assignment. It may take a while, but do not wait until they are perfect before trying to assess them. When you begin to assess your outcomes, you may just discover that you have articulated better outcomes than you thought.

In these examples, satisfaction is no longer being assessed. Assessment is focused on what the program is trying to accomplish and thus what the students are learning and how they are developing. The program's ability to meet these outcomes provides the administrators with helpful information on how to improve their program, restructure their program, or present cases for much-needed resources. In addition, the program's purpose is stated in a way that all constituents know what should be occurring in this program and they know what to expect as a result of their own investment.

Before choosing assessment tools for these outcomes, note that for most cocurricular specialists, it would be unattainable and discouraging to attempt to assess all these outcomes in one year. It may be that a program can see clearly what the logical first outcome would be to assess, or it may be that they assess the outcome that is easiest for them to assess. As mentioned in Chapter Two, the point is to just begin assessing. Remember to take small steps and celebrate your assessment successes, thus encouraging more to become engaged in assessment, as the values of conducting assessment are realized (Table 3–2).

TABLE 3–2

Helpful Reminders
(Source: Bresciani, 2003a.)

- Go ahead and write every program outcome down.
- However, do not try to assess every program outcome every year.
- You may want to start with specific activity outcomes and build program outcomes from those.
- You can start with institutional, division, or unit outcomes and see how your program and activities tie to those.
- Then, move to implementing the entire assessment cycle one outcome at a time, making everything for that systematic—in other words, begin to form "habits" of assessment.
- Remind each other of the benefits of assessment.
- Share examples with each other.
- Celebrate assessment victories.
- Advertise your assessment learnings and decisions made.
- Incorporate students in all facets of assessment planning and implementation, if your program is ready.

Measuring the Student Learning and Development Outcomes

After articulating outcomes, the next step is to consider the manner in which you would evaluate these outcomes. Using the previously mentioned outcome examples, possible assessment methods include self-report surveys, interviews, observations, standardized career service assessment instruments, student portfolios, peer evaluation, and self-evaluation. More information about these methods can be found in the following chapters.

The concept to make note of here is to choose something to evaluate the student learning that may already be inherent in the delivery of the program; but if not inherent, may easily be incorporated into the day-to-day. In addition, this is where you establish the criteria for which you will identify and evaluate. Again, use the previous example outcomes:

- What appropriate interview skills are—meaning you will not only identify what skills you are looking for but also articulate what "appropriate" means.

- What a high level of confidence in their career choice looks like—meaning you will not only identify if the student understands how to make a career choice but also determine what a high level of confidence means. What skills and knowledge are contained in a student's ability to analyze the market and identify at least three types of fields for which they are qualified. What skills and knowledge are contained in a student's ability to document their qualifications for at least three types of positions in their resume and performance portfolios.

Through this type of assessment, it quickly becomes clear how learning and development outcomes can begin to inform decisions for continuous improvement. Through articulating criteria and then observing whether students exhibit the articulated criteria for appropriate interview skills (or the lack thereof), you see for yourself what your students are able to demonstrate. You then can examine your program offerings, looking for holes that should be filled. If you observe that your students are consistently demonstrating the appropriate interview skills, then you are assured that your program is constructed and delivered well and have gathered evidence to share with all your constituents that your program is achieving one aspect that it intends to accomplish. That is evidence worth sharing and celebrating.

The Question of Time

As you can see, this is a time-consuming process (Maki, 2001; Palomba & Banta, 1999). Outcomes are often refined when cocurricular specialists begin to identify how they will evaluate the outcomes. That is all part of the iterative assessment cycle, so there is no need to worry when this type of revision occurs. The purpose of committing time to reflect and plan for assessment is that you examine more carefully the "why" of what you are doing and the "how" you are doing it (Maki, 2002; Palomba & Banta, 1999). When you begin to draft your assessment plan for learning and development, you will most likely see that you were offering programs with unsure end results. You will see how you may be able to reallocate the time from offering those programs for which the end results were unclear to the time involved in assessing the programs for which the end results are clearer (Table 3–3).

There is no new time, and there is rarely any new money. Thus, the following chapters will focus on how you can use existing resources (e.g., time, cocurricular specialists, money, assessment experts, nationally developed assessment tools), reallocated resources, and new resources to implement assessment methods to evaluate student learning and development.

Finally, it may be that a slight change in the delivery of the service needs to occur before assessment of student learning can begin. For example, it may be that the Career Services professionals need to recast their many career services workshops into a curriculum-type model for juniors and seniors. In this curriculum, juniors can begin by drafting their first resume, learning interview etiquette, learning how to research the job markets, and then progress to developing and presenting their portfolios of accomplishments as seniors. A curriculum such as this would allow for more direct methods of assessment, thus producing increased evidence of student learning and development for cocurricular professionals.

TABLE 3–3

Reallocate Your Time and Services
(Source: Bresciani, 2002.)

- In some cases, you may need to recast your services so that you can provide opportunities to assess student development and learning.
- You may even need to offer fewer services so that you can reallocate time to assessment.

Getting off of "Start Here"

If you need some assistance brainstorming ideas that will enable you to write student development and learning outcomes, the following suggestions may prove invaluable. Some places to look for intellectual stimulation include, of course, the documents referenced in Chapter One and the beginning of this chapter.

In addition, the following questions created by Dr. Peggy Maki (2002), senior scholar at the American Association for Higher Education, may also prove helpful in stimulating different ways to approach the writing of your outcomes:

- What do you expect your students to know and be able to do by the end of their education at your institution?

- What do the curricula and the cocurricular "add up to?"

- What do you do in your programs to promote the kinds of learning and development that your institution seeks?

- Which students benefit from which cocurricular experiences?

- What cocurricular processes are responsible for the intended student outcomes the institution seeks?

- How can you help students make connections between classroom learning and experiences outside of the classroom?

- How do you intentionally build upon what each of you hopes to achieve?

The following questions posed by Dr. James A. Anderson (2001a, 2001b), vice-provost for undergraduate affairs at North Carolina State University, may help you recast your services, if needed:

- What are the thinking tasks, intellectual experiences, and/or cocurricula experiences that need to be designed relative to the preparation level and diversity of the students at your institution?

- Can the interpersonal transactions that occur in the everyday life of the student and that reflect cultural orientations serve as a basis for potential new models of critical thinking? What curricular experiences will promote this skill development?

- What structures need to evolve to assure that students have the opportunity to enhance their academic self-concept and understand their role in the culture of learning at your institution?

Also keep in mind, There is value in assessing student satisfaction, needs, and service utilization. There is increased value in assessing student development and learning. In engaging in the latter, you position your program to provide evidence of what you have historically valued as a student affairs and academic support service professional. In addition, you demonstrate your role in the partnership for student learning and development and you illustrate through example your direct contribution to your institutional mission. (Bresciani, 2002, p. 2)

CHAPTER 4

Introduction to Assessment Tools

Choosing a Tool and Method

What is most important when choosing a tool to assess student learning and development is choosing it intentionally. Alexander Astin (1996, p. 132) said "our choice both of student outcomes and of instruments for measuring these outcomes are ultimately based on value judgments." Astin's statement regarding the choice of assessment tools is significant, as there are many tools available to measure the outcomes you articulate for your unit. Carefully considering your options by reflecting on what it is that you want to measure and how you can gather the best evidence is vital to the success of your work. It is also important to note that choosing a tool and implementing it is only one portion of the assessment process. If you are not reading this book in its entirety, it is recommended that you read Chapter Two prior to reading any of the following chapters on special tools to ensure that you have a complete understanding of the assessment process as it is applied in this text, and that you understand where gathering data fits within the continuous assessment cycle.

What Do You Need To Know?

Outcomes-based assessment begins with identifying your unit's or program's mission, objectives and, of course, outcomes. In many cases, it is not easy to identify the best tool(s) for assessment given the complicated nature of your work. It is tempting for those that are trying to fit assessment into already packed workloads to choose a tool without first identifying the specific information to be gathered for improving student learning and development. For example, when a unit is charged with assessing their program for the first time, the response may be, "We will do a survey." While it is not difficult to understand why someone might have

this response, there are at least two problems with this approach. One concern is that this response implies that surveys are "easy." Most people that have created or implemented a survey can tell you it is not as easy as it sounds. Second, there is no consideration of what the unit needs to know about their students when the choice to conduct a survey was made. Administering a survey becomes the assessment process rather than a step in the assessment process.

Thoughtful planning is imperative for successful assessment. After the identification of your unit's mission, objectives, and outcomes, you are ready to gather evidence. But prior to choosing a tool you must ask yourself a series of questions and provide thoughtful answers to each (Table 4–1). After you know the answers to those questions, you can start to think about the most appropriate tools. You can then decide which tool, administered in what way, may be the best choice to measure the outcome(s) identified.

TABLE 4–1

Things to Consider Before Choosing a Tool

1. Which outcome(s) do you want to measure?
2. What do you need to know in order to determine that students know or can do what you have identified in the outcome(s)?
3. Are there set criteria already in place, or do you need to create the criteria?

Other Considerations

It is important to remember that there are other considerations when choosing a tool. Issues such as audience, budget, time frame, analysis capabilities, decision-making factors, and embedding measurements into your regular work activities are all issues that require our attention (Bresciani, 2003a; Ewell, 1985, 1991; Kuh, Douglas, Lund, & Ramin-Gyurnek, 1994; Maki, 2001; Hanson & Bresciani, 2003; Palomba & Banta, 1999; Upcraft & Schuh, 1996). In a perfect world these considerations may not drive our decisions, but they are often a reality for those engaged in assessment. These issues are described more fully in the following paragraphs.

Assessment Audience

In addition to knowing what information you need to gather, you will want to consider whom it is that you are assessing. When assessing student learning in the cocurricular, we are often stumped by the transient nature of our population. This makes choosing the appropriate tool much more difficult. Many units see students one time and have no idea how to identify them. When working with such units on assessment, you are often asked, "How are we supposed to measure what students are learning when we only see them one time?" While that is certainly a difficult situation, there are ways to measure learning and development outcomes with these groups. It may just require some creativity.

In order to plan your assessment, you will want to reflect on whom you are evaluating. When considering this issue, you may want to start with the following questions: What do you know about the students you are trying to assess? Do you know their names and addresses? Do you know how often they attend your programs or use your services? Do you have an opportunity to talk with them prior to or immediately following a program?

Budget

Budget constraints are a reality. Higher education is facing major budget cuts in many states. It is often difficult to find funding for new projects, and assessment activities may fall into a "new" project category. When determining methods and instruments, you should consider the costs. Not only should you consider the cost of the tool, but also the cost of implementation and analysis. With a little training or reading on your own, there are many options that will allow you to create a tool, implement it, and conduct the analysis; and information on tools in future chapters will include low-cost options.

Time Frame

Time, in addition to funding, is one of the most commonly cited reasons for not engaging in assessment. The notion of ensuring that your assessment process is meaningful and manageable is vital to the success of your assessment process. When you are choosing a tool, you might need to consider the length of time involved with creating and implementing it, as well as analyzing the subsequent data. We caution you not to assume that if you are able to hire outside consultants to assist you with parts of your assessment, that you will be able to complete the assessment significantly faster. You will need to work within the consultants' schedules; if you are able to find consultants who can assist you immediately, they will likely want to take the time to understand your organization through multiple contacts. Once the consultants begin constructing something for your unit, you will want to have regular contact to ensure that what they are creating meets your needs.

Analysis Capabilities

Choosing a tool to gather data must include reflection on how the data will be analyzed and by whom. Imagine a situation in which you spent precious time creating a wonderful survey to measure a specified set of outcomes but then realized you had no way to analyze the data. It is likely that the result would be high frustration and possibly unexpected costs to hire someone else to conduct the data analysis. The lesson is to make sure, prior to committing any resources to a tool or method, that you know how you will have the data analyzed. If you do not know how to analyze the data yourself and choose not to learn, make sure you consult whomever you need to in order to have a data analysis plan in place so that the raw data are not simply put away and never used.

Reporting of Results and Decisions

A key to meaningful assessment is using the data you collect to make decisions for continuous improvement. The desired outcome is to determine if students are learning what you say they are, and if they are not, make improvements in the program so that they will. When choosing an instrument, it is important to be certain that the type of information you gather will help you make improvements. Reflection on how the information will assist you in making decisions is critical when choosing instruments.

Who Will Need To See The Data?

When you are using data to support decisions, it is entirely possible that others will need to see the data as well. Supervisors or other administrators may request to see the data that support a change or request for funding. It is important to consider who will see the data and, if possible, determine the types of data to which they will respond most positively. Some people respond better to empirical data, while others are more interested in rich data that result from interviews or focus groups. Regardless of the type of data you use, be sure to include the justification for your choice in your documentation and, if possible, collect data from different sources to make an even more meaningful point.

Direct Verses Indirect Data

Keeping in mind the issues raised above, you might consider whether the data you gather need to be direct evidence or indirect evidence of learning and development. Palomba and Banta (1999) define "direct evidence" as methods of collecting information that require the students to display their knowledge and skills, and "indirect evidence" as methods that ask students or someone else to reflect on the student learning. While both types of data are helpful, there may be more value in providing direct evidence of learning and development verses providing information indicating that students say they are learning and developing. This will depend on the data use and the constituents to whom it is reported.

An Example of Indirect Data that are Meaningful

When surveys are used as tools to assess competencies they can generate indirect data that are meaningful in terms of students' improvement over a period of time. Such surveys can be adjusted to the needs of the population that will be surveyed. Tacoma Community College has beta tested a version of their Living and Working Co-operatively surveys. These surveys are structured to measure students' perceptions of teamwork, diversity in society, and their roles as members of the multicultural community of the classroom. The sequencing of the surveys is structured to reveal students' improvement in these competencies over a quarter and the success of the instructional techniques in achieving these goals.

The first survey, the Baseline Survey, is given during the first few days of the quarter and serves to provide a tool for the students to begin to focus on the Living and Working Co-operatively competency within the context of the classroom. The second survey, the Follow-Up Survey, given during the second week of the quarter, seeks to reinforce the serious nature of developing skills in this competency. The third survey, the Mid-Quarter survey, focuses on the development of the substructure of the competency within the classroom. The fourth survey, the Summative Survey, is done during the last two weeks of the quarter and focuses on the students' actual knowledge and skills so that students can self-assess their development in this competency over the quarter.

Instructors are encouraged to use the surveys in conjunction with graded assignments, such as:

- writing a one-minute paragraph answer about the value of diversity,
- writing an essay clarifying their survey responses,
- writing an essay about diversity or the process of learning this competency,
- summarizing or otherwise keeping track of the student's individual development via a journal or other method, and
- presenting a reflector's report about some aspect of living and working cooperatively to the class.

Although this survey is not a direct or authentic indicator of student learning of a competency, it serves as an effective tool in the indirect assessment of an outcome within the classroom.

Fit into responsibilities

The length of time associated with the assessment cycle, while always continuous, may vary by outcome and by measure of the outcome. Based on the type of assessment, the group being assessed, and other issues, some measures will occur every five years, some every year, and some everyday. Regardless of how often you plan to measure an outcome, considering how you can incorporate it into your regular workload ensures that the cycle will continue. It may be necessary to make changes to a program or practice to allow for easier assessment. For example, asking people to sign in when they attend an event may allow for easier follow up. Another example is to restructure current satisfaction surveys to include questions that would allow students to provide direct or self-reported evidence of their learning and development.

Sharing Data

One way to address several of the aforementioned issues is to combine assessment efforts with other units or programs. While this may assist in reducing costs and require less time from each of the individual units or programs, it is possible that sharing data may cause other issues to arise. Not only would careful negotiations regarding methodology, costs, and workload need to be addressed prior to the assessment, but also issues regarding confidentiality of the findings and use of the data would need to be considered.

Information on Tools

In an attempt to provide practitioners with the appropriate foundations for a wide variety of assessment activities, we discuss a range of tools. Some tools are used more often and are more commonly accepted, while others are less used in the cocurricular professions yet are of equal value. You will find discussions on the Council for the Advancement of Standards in Higher Education process, best practices, performance indicators, benchmarking, peer reviews and external reviews, interviews and focus groups, observations and document analysis, case studies, analyzing qualitative data, survey research, and portfolios.

Although the structure of the chapters may vary slightly based on the topic, each section will include:

- descriptions of the tool or method,

- the purposes and uses of these tools or methods,

- example outcomes,

- basic implementation tips,

- issues to consider in order to create or adapt the tool for your own assessment plan, and

- cost-savings tips.

In addition to chapters on tools for assessing learning and development, there are chapters on strategies for analyzing data. Through the various tools and analysis chapters, it is our sincere hope that you find the information that you need to engage in meaningful assessment of student learning and development. While the following chapters provide an overview, it is not our intent to provide comprehensive information on each tool or method, as that is not possible in this text. Each tool or method has its own body of literature, and you are encouraged to explore those resources to inform your work.

CHAPTER 5

Criteria and Rubrics

Introduction

Throughout Chapters Two and Three, you have seen the word "criteria" used. Similar to many other terms throughout this book, it has various meanings. Merriam-Webster (2003) defines criteria as **"1:** a standard on which a judgment or decision may be based **2 :** a characterizing mark or trait" (http://www.m-w.com/cgi-bin/dictionary). For purposes of this chapter, we refer to criteria as the set of indicators, markers, guides, or a list of measures or qualities that will help you know when a student has met an outcome. For example, take the outcome, *students will demonstrate excellent oral communication when presenting their agendas to the student senate,* and assume that we have applied the questions from Chapter Two to this outcome. We have asked and answered, "Is it measurable? Is it meaningful? Is it manageable? Who will I be gathering evidence from to know that my outcome has been met? Who would know if my outcome has been met?"

Now, we begin to ask, "How will I know if it has been met? Will it provide me with evidence that will lead me to make a decision for continuous improvement?" In order to answer these two questions, we need to identify some criteria. What does *excellent oral communication* look like? Fortunately, there is a wealth of literature on excellent oral communication (See http://www2.chass.ncsu.edu/CWSP/resources/publications.html for references.). The combination of this literature, as well as your own professional expertise, and the expertise leveraged from your faculty and administrative colleagues will allow you to begin to design a list of criteria that will help you identify when students are making decisions and what it looks like when they are making them.

Example criteria for the outcome (*students will demonstrate excellent oral communication when presenting their*

agendas to the student senate) could include a listing of what to look for in the presenter. For example, the presenter:

- speaks in a clear voice;
- engages the audience;
- uses appropriate rates of speech;
- uses culturally appropriate eye contact;
- does not exhibit nervous habits;
- is dressed appropriately;
- maintains appropriate posture;
- provides audience with ample time to ask questions;
- is well organized;
- includes a clear beginning, middle, and end to the presentation;
- uses a strong organizing theme with clear main ideas and transitions;
- includes complete information;
- incorporates accurate information;
- uses appropriate and meaningful visual aids;
- uses attractive handouts; and
- pays attention to the length of allotted time.

This set of criteria provides all constituents with a better understanding of what it looks like when *students demonstrate excellent oral communication when presenting their agendas to the student senate.*

Another example outcome may be, *students will collaborate when planning student cultural activities.* Ask the questions,

"How will I know if it has been met? Will it provide me with evidence that will lead me to make a decision for continuous improvement?" Using the approach illustrated in the aforementioned paragraph, you can adapt a rubric developed from researchers involved with the National Biological Service Carbrillo Tidepool Study and come up with the following list of criteria, based on scholarly literature (see http://edweb.sdsu.edu/triton/tidepoolunit/Rubrics/collrubric.html).

Collaboration means that students will:

- research information,

- gather information,

- share information,

- be punctual for meetings,

- fulfill their assigned job responsibility,

- volunteer to assist others when their work is complete,

- participate in their assigned cultural activity,

- listen to other teammates (e.g., committee members), and

- make fair decisions.

In these examples, you are viewing only a list of criteria, but the listing helps students understand what is expected of them. The criteria listing also helps the program administrators know what to teach the students, and it helps the administrators to identify whether the students have met the intended outcomes. Where students do not meet the intended outcome, the program administrators know precisely what to improve or at least have more direction in which to make decisions and recommendations for improvement.

So, why bother with a rubric?

What is a Rubric?

A rubric is "a set of criteria and a scoring scale that is used to assess and evaluate students' work. Often rubrics identify levels or ranks with criteria indicated for each level" (Campbell, Melenyzer, Nettles, & Wyman, 2000, p. 283.). Huba and Freed (2000) define a rubric as that which "explains to students the criteria against which their work will be judged. More importantly for our purposes, it makes public, key criteria that students can use in developing, revising, and judging their own work" (p. 155).

You will note that the word "rubric" cannot be defined without referencing criteria. Simply put, rubrics are an expansion of criteria. When only a list of criteria is used to evaluate an outcome, there is an absence or a presence of the outcome's existence, or that which defines the outcome. The one evaluating whether the criteria exists is the one, for example, forming judgments about whether the *student has used a strong organizing theme with clear main ideas and transitions, has included complete information, or has incorporated accurate information*. While the listing of criteria gives more meaning to the outcome of *students will demonstrate excellent oral communication*, there is still plenty of subjectivity left to the evaluator. This is not a "bad" thing, but it does make it a little less clear for the student and the program administrators to know where the "target" of their learning is and thus, what needs to be improved in order for them to either demonstrate that they have learned it or to know what else needs to be learned.

In addition to the list of criteria, rubrics provide descriptive levels of achievement (Beauchamp, Parsons, & Sanford, 1996; Huba & Freed, 2000; Popham, 1997) or describe varying levels of performance or dimensions of quality. In other words, rather than just stating whether the criteria exists or not (e.g., *yes* or *no* or *excellent* or *poor*), rubrics typically define in more detail the levels of achievement. In addition, instead of stating that a student demonstrated the learning at a level of *excellent* or *poor, excellent* is described in detail for what the evaluator was looking to find. *Poor* is defined as well, as would any other middle achievement levels of the outcome that the evaluator would expect to see. While the process of making human judgments can never be completely standardized," (Huba & Freed, 2000, p. 172), rubrics help define student and cocurricular specialists' expectations for student learning and development.

Why Use a Rubric?

There are several reasons to use a rubric as an evaluation method (Andrade, 2000; Huba & Freed, 2000; Popham, 1997). Table 5–1 briefly lists some of these reasons. Furthermore, a rubric:

- Provides evaluators and those whose work is being evaluated with rich and detailed descriptions of what is being learned and what is not.

- Combats accusations that evaluators do not know what they are looking for in learning and development.

- Can be used as a teaching tool—students begin to understand what it is they are or are not learning, and are or are not able to demonstrate what they know and can do. When students begin to see what they are not learning, they can take more responsibility for their learning.

- Teaches students the standards of the discipline or the standards of the cocurricular learning and development experience.

- Allows students to help set the standards of their performance for an outcome.

- Allows students to evaluate themselves and their peers.

For example, you can use a rubric to:

- <u>Norm faculty and cocurricular specialists expectations.</u> As previously mentioned, if faculty and cocurricular specialists join together to precisely articulate criteria and levels of performance for student learning and development, they can then work more diligently on improving the programs that would provide such learning and development experiences, because the faculty and cocurricular specialists share the desired learning and development outcome.

- <u>Inform students of what you are looking for.</u> As previously mentioned, if you can explain in detail to students what they are expected to get out of a particular experience or series of activities, the students begin to see the value in the activity and can then assist in their own evaluations as well as assume greater responsibility for their own performances.

- <u>Give students an opportunity to see how they have improved.</u> If you have applied the same or similar rubric over the course of a semester, year, or a student's academic career and you have articulated well the varying levels, students may be able to clearly see how they have progressed in their oral presentation skills or problem-solving abilities.

- <u>Make rankings, ratings, and grades more meaningful.</u> For those of you who assign grades to your cocurricular activities, even if it was simply *pass* or *fail*, putting your grading criteria into a rubric allows you and the students to better understand why they are receiving a particular

grade. Students begin to understand what they have "missed" and what they have yet to learn. This same philosophy can be applied to employee evaluations. Doing so also helps protect against the bias that may easily enter into evaluations and grading.

- <u>Help students identify their own learning and development or absence thereof.</u>

- <u>Assess a student, activity, or a program.</u> A rubric can be used to evaluate an individual student's learning and development, or it can be applied holistically to evaluate the learning of all students from a particular activity or program. One rubric may even be applied to evaluate student learning across several programs. For example, if faculty and cocurricular specialists collaborate to create a problem-solving rubric or teamwork rubric, then they may be able to adapt and apply the rubric across various units, for a variety of activities, to assess problem solving or group collaboration.

TABLE 5–1

Uses for Rubric

You can use a rubric to:

- norm faculty and cocurricular specialists' expectations;
- inform students of what you are looking for in their work;
- give students an opportunity to see how they have improved;
- make rankings, ratings, and grades more meaningful;
- help students identify their own learning and development or absence thereof; and
- assess a student, activity, or a program.

Types of Rubrics

In order to understand the use of rubrics and criteria, we will illustrate various types of rubrics (e.g., checklist, advanced checklist, simple model, full model) and their potential application to one outcome. It may be helpful to think of this as an evolutionary developmental process, as the following example has evolved for us over several years. However, the purpose of this exercise is not to demean the use of criteria listings; rather, the purpose is to illustrate that there are ways and reasons to use one over the other. The beauty of being the practitioner assessment cocurricular specialist is that you and your colleagues get to decide what will work best for your program(s). In addition, you may decide to begin with a criteria listing and then develop the detailed descriptions of levels over time. Again, we remind you that this chapter is fundamental and introductory in nature. More sophisticated scholarly information can be found in the references at the end of this book.

The outcome used for the following example is, *resident advisors will be able to identify and explain reasons for ethical dilemmas in relationships found in residence hall roommates.*

The Checklist

The checklist is a simple list of criteria and the possible inclusion of a rating scale. An example follows.

1. 2-minute description of ethical dilemma   _____

2. Explanation of ethical dilemma   _____

3. Explanation of reason for ethical dilemma   _____

4. Depth of awareness of potential barriers to resolving ethical dilemma   _____

5. Illustration of expected results in resolving dilemma   _____

In this example, the evaluator could rate the student with a Y = Yes and N = No or 4 = Excellent and 1 = Poor. You can also see in this example that this list of criteria most likely assesses more than this one stated outcome. Or it could be perceived that the checklist is "step-like" in nature and assumes that some of these criteria must be present in order for the outcome to be met. Setting up a checklist in this manner assists the program administrators with knowing what went well and what did not. This provides information to make decisions for continuous improvement.

One important benefit of this tool is that it is quick to use. The hall director could use this checklist when the resident advisor is reporting a conflict either in person (which is what this was designed for) or in writing (which would require a bit of adaptation). The challenge to this evaluation tool is that neither the evaluator nor the student being evaluated may understand the extent of the quality of their *explanation* or the *depth of their awareness.* Regardless, this quick checklist can help hall directors gauge whether they are doing a good job educating their resident advisors to identify, analyze,

explain reasons for ethical dilemmas among residents, and apply interventions.

Advanced Checklist

Advanced checklists include fuller descriptions of the list of criteria and a rating scale. In the following example you see only one portion of the rubric, criteria number 2. (The rest of the rubric includes the other criteria stated in the first example with similar elongated descriptions for each criterion.) Note that the description of the criteria is expanded, even though the description of levels remains fairly simplistic.

> Criteria number 2: Explanation of reason for ethical dilemma.
> The student should be able to identify that the reasons for the dilemma may vary and may be associated with the student's identity, personal beliefs, and values.
>
> Rate the student using the following scale:
> 3 = Excellent
> 2 = Good
> 1 = Poor

Simple Model

The simple model includes a fuller description of the list of criteria as well as simple descriptions of the levels of mastery. Similar to the previous example, in the following example you see only one portion of the rubric, criteria number 2. (The rest of the rubric includes the other criteria stated in the first example with similar elongated descriptions for each criteria and the rating scale.)

> Criteria number 2: Explanation of reason for ethical dilemma.
> The student should be able to identify that the reasons for the dilemma may vary and may be associated with the student's identity, personal beliefs, and values. The student should also demonstrate that as the evaluator he/she could not assume identification of the reasons for the ethical dilemma.
>
> Rate the student using the following scale:
> 4 = Excellent ability to identify multiple reasons, with no assumptions
>
> 3 = Good ability to identify multiple reasons, with some assumptions
>
> 2 = Poor ability to identify multiple reasons, with assumptions

1 = No ability to identify multiple reasons, with many assumptions

Full Model

The full model contains the fullest descriptions of the list of criteria and more complete descriptions of the levels of mastery. Here, the intent is to get as detailed as possible so that the rubric can be applied by students to students, as well as applied by cocurricular specialists in other units. In addition, with this level of detail, the cocurricular specialist can even expect the student to self-evaluate their work. Again, similar to the previous example, in the following example you see only one portion of the rubric, criteria number 2. In addition, you are only viewing one detailed description from the scale, the exemplary level or level number 4. (The rest of the rubric includes the other criteria stated in the first example with similar elongated descriptions for each criterion and detailed descriptions of the rating scale.)

Criteria number 2: Explanation of reason for ethical dilemma.

The student should be able to identify that the reasons for the dilemma may vary and may be associated with the student's (experiencing the ethical dilemma) identity, personal beliefs, and values. The student should also demonstrate that identification of the reasons might not be assumed based on any bio-demographic characteristics of the student (experiencing the ethical dilemma). In addition, the student should be able to succinctly articulate the reasons for the ethical dilemma.

An example from the scale:

4 = *Exemplary*

The student demonstrated the ability to identify multiple reasons for the ethical dilemma, with no assumptions. In other words, the student was able to detach the reasons from the student's (experiencing the ethical dilemma) bio-demographic characteristics. Furthermore, the report given by the student is succinct, clear, and detailed, as is his/her recommendation for corrective and educational action.

Using Criteria to Assess the Impact of Leadership on Diversity: A Practical Example

Before illustrating how to design a rubric, we provide you with another example of its use. Historically, the primary vehicles of assessment for cocurricular programs and academic support services have been student

satisfaction surveys, reviews of programs and services by external parties, and competitive benchmarking (reviewing exemplary services and programs of other peer organizations). While such approaches can yield valuable information, they do not allow the organization to take an intimate look at itself.

Spanbauer (1996) discusses the more recent attempts to measure the quality and effectiveness of student service activities. These involve the development of survey instruments using a set of criteria as a basis for measurement. The philosophy underlying this type of assessment is the focus on continuous improvement. Two examples of such assessments are: (1) the Student Satisfaction Inventory produced by the USA Group Noel-Levitz and (2) the Campus Quality Survey designed by the USA Group National Quality Academy. The results of such assessments should be reviewed relative to the "total quality improvement" criteria that are used.

Several attempts have been made to translate the Malcolm Baldrige Examination Criteria to education. The two aforementioned surveys are examples of this type of survey extrapolation. The power of such assessments involves the use of criteria that emerge out of consensual conversations about standards, quality, and effectiveness. When these criteria are coupled with insightful questions, the assessment process can become very powerful. Appendix A incorporates a modification of the Baldrige criteria. The instrument attempts to examine organizational leadership as it applies to the implementation of "diversity" throughout the organization.

Steps to Creating a Rubric

As mentioned in the *Introduction to Tools* chapter, there are some very specific questions that one should answer prior to choosing a tool. When considering rubrics, the following are most important to consider (also see Table 5–2):

1) Articulate the outcome you wish to assess. Thus, prior to creating a rubric, choose the outcome you wish to assess with a rubric.

2) Decide what meeting the outcome looks like. Ask yourself, "How do you know the outcome has been met? What does it look like?" This is key, as you need to articulate exactly what you are looking for and how you will know it has been met. As mentioned in the examples, there is usually a wealth of scholarly literature that can be referenced to assist you with articulating how you

know your outcome will be met. In addition, leveraging the knowledge of your faculty colleagues and your fellow cocurricular specialists (e.g., the folks who have been doing it for years and know what it looks like when they see it) is extremely wise and valuable.

3) <u>While step 3 may come before step 2, depending on how you write your outcome, be sure that you have identified how you will be collecting evidence that the outcome has been met.</u> For example, articulating criteria for the outcome, *students will be able to demonstrate problem-solving skills as tutorial assistants,* may depend on how you plan for the students to provide you with evidence that they have demonstrated problem-solving skills. Do you want to have them write essays about how they are identifying the problem learning issues of their tutees, and then design and apply a problem-solving rubric to evaluate the essays? Or do you want to be able to observe the tutors and apply the rubric to their tutoring sessions? Or would you prefer that the student use the rubric to self-evaluate after a tutoring session? Or would you prefer that the student being tutored evaluate the tutor after a series of tutoring sessions? In either choice, making sure that you have identified an opportunity or opportunities to gather the evidence is extremely important prior to designing the rubric levels in order to assess a student's ability to distinguish *problem definition* in writing verses in a one-on-one tutoring session. The demonstration of the learning may look very different depending on the situation you are asking them to supply evidence for.

4) <u>Place the descriptions into a listing of criteria.</u> If you need help with this, it may prove beneficial to have one of your colleagues sit and listen to you describe what it looks like when students *can articulate ways to prevent disease and speed recovery from illness.* Your colleague can list the themes or key words he/she hears you describe. This can begin to form a list of criteria that you will check later with the scholarly literature. It may be interesting to note that this is a typical "sticking point" when designing rubrics. Often, we witness that cocurricular specialists do not trust themselves to articulate what they have known for years and what they do know because they are the expert in

identifying what they want students to be able to know and do in their particular programs. They are experts because they have read and applied the literature, have learned from their students, and have engaged in ongoing professional development. So, trust yourself, write it down. You will have plenty of time for it to be critiqued and improved by your cocurricular and academic colleagues.

5) <u>Once you have your list of criteria, you may want to begin to expand it into the more detailed descriptions of the criteria—that is, if you choose to use the expanded checklist, simple model, or full model rubric design.</u> Even if you maintain the simple checklist, it may be helpful for you to describe the criteria in one or two sentences so that when you norm your colleagues or students to apply the rubric, they have a better understanding of what you are expecting to identify.

6) <u>Choose a model for a rubric that bests fits your project.</u> Here is where you choose from the aforementioned models or make up your own model. It matters less which you choose; it matters more that you are engaging in assessment. The URLs referenced at the end of the chapter may be able to help you if you get stuck with model design choice.

7) <u>Articulate the number of levels and the type of level you would expect for the criteria to be demonstrated.</u> When choosing the number of levels, you can choose two, three, or four. The point is to be able to discriminate against what a level one looks like, verses a level two, or a level three, or a level four. We often defer to the wisdom of one of our colleagues, John Tector, associate dean in the College of Design at North Carolina State University. Tector believes that most human beings can only differentiate three levels of anything—"It is not there," "sort of there," and "all there." We tend to agree with Tector and, therefore, most of our rubrics have three levels. Here, you can choose a simple rating scale or begin to describe in detail what you are looking for and what various levels look like. If you get stuck here, just think about the various levels in which you have seen students' abilities reside prior to your decision to use a rubric. The descriptions may come more easily with past observations of students' learning in mind. If not, ask your colleagues and even students to assist you. Again, it may be more meaningful for

you to start out with a rating scale and develop the description of the levels over years of using the rubric. That is how we have developed the majority of the rubrics we use. Other helpful tips we have used include sharing our rubric with our faculty colleague who is a rhetorician or with our faculty colleague who is a technical writer. Mike Carter and Jo Allen have helped us refine many performance levels and criteria descriptions, as their mastery of language and communication ability is so much more sophisticated than our own.

8) Norm the group using the rubric. While this, again, is a simplified version of the denotation of the word "norm," the purpose here is to get everyone on the same page as to the meaning of the criteria and as to the identification of the varying levels that they may see students demonstrate. When a group of colleagues work together to create or refine a rubric, they often begin the norming process because there is debate and discussion about what the criteria should be and what they look like when a student has mastered them. It is a wonderfully exciting process in which to be a part or facilitate. It is even more exhilarating when students are allowed to play a role in the creation of the rubric. Finally, sometimes it is helpful to create a piece of work that you expect represents certain criteria and certain levels so that you can see if the "targeted" learning can be met and if you will all recognize it when you see it.

9) Pilot the rubric. Test the rubric either on a pilot group of students, on some previous student work (although that may be difficult because people usually find they change the delivery of the service or program that created an artifact of learning after they have created a rubric, and thus the previous artifacts may not be appropriate to use), or on some colleagues willing to role-play as students.

10) Revise the rubric. Mindful that assessment is an iterative process, so are the tools that allow you to gather the evidence of student learning and development. We refine our rubrics every year because the students help us to better communicate the criteria and the levels of expected performance. There may be one day when we do not have to further refine our rubrics, but we have not yet reached that point.

TABLE 5−2

Steps to Creating a Rubric

- Articulate the outcome you wish to assess with the rubric.
- Decide what meeting the outcome looks like— "How do you know the outcome has been met? What does it look like?"
- Identify the activity in which you will be gathering the evidence of student learning (e.g., essay, activity, observation).
- Articulate exactly what you are looking for and how you will know it has been met.
- List the aforementioned as criteria or a detailed description.
- Choose a model for a rubric that bests fits your project. Articulate the levels you would expect that criteria to be demonstrated.
- If you choose, define those levels in great detail.
- Norm the group using the rubric.
- Pilot the rubric.
- Revise the rubric.

Basic Agreements

Rubrics are a wonderful way to assess the student population that may flow in and out of your program and into another cocurricular specialist's area. For example, while we have no empirical data on this, it appears that on various campuses the same students who are involved in student government are also resident advisors or orientation leaders, or Greek leaders or peer advisors. As such, we may not be able to have these students long enough to assess what they have learned from us, or we may only capture a point in their learning and development and then they move onto another cocurricular specialist's program. Thus, using similar rubrics across programs for problem solving, collaboration, reflection, and other such shared outcomes may be possible, if all can agree on some basic criteria and levels of performance.

When using the same rubric across programs, units, or division lines, it is important to have some basic conformity. Following are some basic agreements that are advantageous to have in place when sharing rubrics across organizational lines:

- Agree on the outcome you are assessing with the rubric.

- Agree on a method of data collection such as an essay or presentation.

- Agree on the meaning for the outcome and definition. In other words, agree on how you know the outcome is met and what it will look like when you see it met.

- Agree on the systematic implementation of the assignments, activities, projects, and the rubric.

Implementing the Rubric

In many ways, some of the implementation issues for rubrics have been addressed in the instructions on designing the rubric (Table 5–3). Following is a recap:

- Remind the rubric users of the outcome being assessed.

- Remind the rubric users about how the evidence for the outcome will be collected (e.g., activity, project assignment, presentation, essay, portfolio report).

- Norm the group that is using the rubric to evaluate sample evidence.

- Pilot the rubric on the sample work.

- Revise the rubric to make it most meaningful to the users.

- Make sure those who are using the rubric and those whose work is being evaluated with the rubric understand all of its dimensions.

- Revise, revise, and revise.

- Make the rubric public. This is a controversial suggestion. Some evaluators believe that the rubric should not be made public for it appears to be "teaching to the test." Others argue that making the rubric public means that students can better take responsibility for what is expected of them and that program administrators become more accountable for what is expected of them. The purpose of our including this as an implementation step is to illustrate that we believe making the rubric public has great value for both the student and the cocurricular professional delivering the learning. Not only is it valuable for the aforementioned reasons, but also because it does not "teach to the test." A rubric describes what the demonstrated learning and development looks like. It does not mean that the leaning and development cannot be more that what is stated on the rubric. If rubrics are written well with developmental theory in mind, rubrics can be invaluable to everyone understanding the interrelatedness of learning and development. Thus, we highly recommend making the rubrics public.

- Fully incorporate the rubric and the artifacts you are assessing with it into your assessment plan.

TABLE 5–3

Questions to Ask and Actions to Implement for Developing Useful Rubrics
(Source: Adapted from Huba & Freed, 2000.)

Question	Action
1. What criteria or essential elements must be present in the student's work to know that the outcome has been met?	Place each criterion in rows on the far left side of your rubric.
2. How many levels of quality do I think we can identify in the student's ability to meet each criteria?	Include these as columns in your rubric, and label them with the description of the level. You should have as many columns as you have levels.
3. For each criterion, what is a clear description of what a particular level of performance or achievement looks like?	Include detailed descriptions of the accomplishment of each criterion in the appropriate performance level cells of the rubric.
4. When I use the rubric, what aspects work well and what aspects need improvement?	Revise, revise, and revise.

Analyzing and Reporting Information Gathered from a Rubric

Many people are not interested in using rubrics because they think it is qualitative information and that qualitative data will not be the type of information that will influence their constituents. Data collected from rubrics is qualitative in nature, thus allowing for the rich educational purpose of the data and for the meaningful information that will lead to the improvement of programs. However, this does not mean that one cannot assign number values to each rubric cell in order to turn qualitative information into numeric information for those constituents who respond well to numerical data.

Prior to illustrating how you can turn rich meaningful descriptive data into numbers, let's first explore how you could summarize the detailed descriptions for reporting and decision-making. For example,

- Report, in narrative form, where individual students fell into each rubric cell, what you concluded based on those individual student learning analysis, and what decisions and recommendations you have for your program and others based on that analysis.

- Summarize which categories students primarily were in, providing examples of the rubric cell as it is applied to the demonstrated learning of the criteria. Then, discuss how you interpret that information in regards to student learning and development, illustrating decisions and recommendations for improvement.

- Summarize which categories students were in, using percentages to classify levels and criteria competencies. Then, discuss how you interpret that information with regards to student learning and development, listing decisions and recommendations for improvement.

- You can use the criteria in the rubric to holistically evaluate where students are in their learning and development and to determine the resulting decisions and recommendations. For example,

when working with one group of evaluators, they were uncomfortable placing the students' performance into cells; rather, they used the rubric to norm their expectations and reported demonstrated strengths and areas of improvement for the group as a whole.

- You can assign numeric values to each cell, analyze the students individually or holistically, grouping them into cells, adding the scores of the cells, and converting the scores to 1.0–4.0 scale or to a 1–100 scale or anything in between that has meaning. An example of this type of rubric can be found in Appendix B.

TABLE 5–4

Cost-saving Tips

Rubrics are low cost in dollars to design and implement. The investment in rubrics is in scholarly research time, conversation time among evaluators and students, and in norming, should that be pursued. Resource-saving tips include:

1) Visiting these websites to garner easily adaptable ideas from K-12 assessment professionals:
   - http://school.discovery.com/schrockguide/assess.html
   - http://www.odyssey.on.ca/~elaine.coxon/rubrics.htm
   - http://rubistar.4teachers.org/
   - http://intranet.cps.k12.il.us/Assessments/
     Ideas_and_Rubrics/ideas_and_rubrics.html
     http://teachers.teach-nology.com/web_tools/rubrics/

2) Sharing rubrics with your colleagues. For example, if more than one of you is assessing problem solving, ask one of your colleagues to work with you and a team of faculty to develop a rubric that you can adapt. Meanwhile, offer to share the rubric you created with them.

3) See http://www.ncsu.edu/undergrad_affairs/assessment/files/evaluation/uapr_process_evaluation_rubric.htm for an example of a rubric that can be adapted to assess your student learning and development outcomes.

CHAPTER 6

The Council for the Advancement of Standards in Higher Education

Description

There are very few units within the cocurricular that have certification or accreditation programs. It is more common to find that programs have standards set for them by national organizations. The American College Personnel Association (ACPA) and the National Association of Student Personnel Administrators (NASPA) developed the Council for the Advancement of Standards in Higher Education (CAS) in 1979 to provide quality assurance in cocurricular programs. CAS enlisted the assistance of professionals from a variety of programs to create standards and guidelines for 29 functional areas. These standards and guidelines are located in the Self-Assessment Guide (SAG) for each functional area. There are standards and guidelines for the following functional areas: Academic Advising; Admissions Programs; Alcohol and Other Drug Programs; Campus Activities; Campus Information and Visitor Services; Career Services; College Health Programs; College Unions; Commuter Student Programs; Conference and Events Standards; Counseling Services; Disability Services; Educational Services for Distance Learners; Financial Aid Programs; Fraternity and Sorority Advising; Housing and Residential Life Programs; International Student Programs; Judicial Programs; Leadership Programs; Learning Assistance Programs; Lesbian, Gay, Bisexual, and Transgender Programs; Orientation Programs; Minority Student Programs; Outcomes Assessment and Program Evaluation; Recreational Sports Programs; Registrar Programs and Services; Religious Programs; TRIO and Other Educational Opportunity Programs; Women Student Programs; and Masters Level Student

Affairs Administration Preparation Programs (Miller, 1999, p. iii).

CAS has developed professional standards and guidelines for these programs to aspire to and promote self-assessment and self-regulation. The general subjects reviewed are in the areas of mission, program (which includes providing evidence of student learning), leadership, organization and management, human resources, financial resources, facilities, technology and equipment, legal responsibilities, equity and access, campus and community relations, diversity, ethics, and assessment and evaluation (Miller, 1999). The standards are considered minimum requirements for good practice and the guidelines are more specific statements that enhance and enrich programs (Miller, 1999).

Example Outcomes

While the CAS process can be implemented institution wide, for the purposes of this book we will review the process at the program or unit level. There are several ways to incorporate the CAS process into an existing continuous assessment plan. The SAG standards and guidelines could be used as a tool to support the meeting of an outcome, or each standard can be an outcome for a program. For example, in order to make their assessment plan more manageable, the Office of Student Conduct (OSC) at NC State University used the Judicial Program SAG standards as a form of measurement for one outcome. The outcome listed in the plan was to meet the standards for Judicial Programs. This outcome was one of several designed to meet the objective of improving credibility of the OSC. In addition to measuring this outcome, the program outcomes for the office were added to the SAG standards and measured with the standards. While there may have been some degree of overlap between the OSC program outcomes taken from their assessment plan and the SAG standards for Judicial Programs, the OSC staff believed that their program outcomes, as articulated by the staff, were important enough to review in multiple sections of the CAS process. Two examples of such outcomes are "Staff in the OSC will develop partnerships with other offices to promote professional development of OSC staff" and "Staff in the OSC offer information about services, the Honor Code, and procedures through our web page."

Implementing the CAS process and then using the information gathered to inform change completed the cycle for that outcome. The OSC's Assessment Plan includes reassessing the SAG standards in approximately five years. While the actual impact of the activity on credibility has not yet been measured, the ability to let faculty and staff on campus know that the OSC meets the professional standards determined by CAS is believed to assist in improving credibility.

CAS has developed a learning and development component to the professional standards. As part of the self-study, programs will have the opportunity to use some of the methods described in this book to measure learning and development outcomes as part of the CAS General Standards. CAS will provide example outcomes for those that have not identified learning and development outcomes at the time of their self-study. Adding learning and development outcomes to the process will allow programs to conduct more complete self-studies that not only demonstrate that they met national standards set by professional organizations, but also demonstrate the impact of their program on student learning and development.

Implementation

One of the many benefits of the CAS process is that there is a clearly outlined implementation process. When a unit orders a SAG for their functional area, instructions for implementation of the CAS process are included. The process, while not without challenge, is straightforward and the end result is valuable feedback from a variety of constituents.

Implementation is a five-step process that includes developing a team of reviewers, understanding classifications, compiling documentation, assigning ratings, and implementing change. A brief description of each step follows, but those interested in participating in a CAS review should read the full descriptions as provided in the CAS materials that can be purchased at http://www.cas.edu/.

Developing a Team
CAS recommends identifying a leader for the process. Ideally, the leader should be someone that can coordinate the review process. The leader may be a member of your staff or someone from another unit. The team members should include students, faculty, staff, and representatives from other groups of constituents, and the size of the group should range from three to five. The staff implementing the self-study should train the team regarding the CAS standards and guidelines being assessed, the process, inter-rater reliability, and any other relevant issues. While identifying a team may sound like a simple task, it may be difficult to find individuals that are willing to devote time to your assessment. You might consider "trading" opportunities to assist with assessment projects with individuals from other units.

Understanding Classification
The SAG for each functional area includes standards and guidelines. As defined previously, standards are considered the minimum for best practice and guidelines are additional suggested outcomes that are indicators of comprehensive practice. Standards include the word "must" or "shall," and guidelines include the word "may." The staff in the unit or the assessment team should determine if the unit will be assessed using the standards, standards and some guidelines, or all the standards and guidelines. There may be times when a standard is not appropriate for a unit based on any number of issues. Such standards should be identified prior to the actual assessment. An example of a standard that was considered not appropriate for the OSC was "Interns and others in training who work in the program are qualified by enrollment in an appropriate field of study and relevant experience." The office did not have any "Interns and others in training" at the time of the review.

Compiling Documentation
The unit must provide the review team evidence of all standards in written form. This evidence may be in the form of web pages, office forms, reports, handbooks, employee resumes, evaluations, student files, e-mails, or any other relevant document. Collecting the necessary documentation may be a long and tedious process, but

it is the foundation for the review. Without proper documentation, the reviewers are not able to effectively rate the unit.

Assigning Ratings

Reviewers will be asked to assign ratings to each standard and guideline used in the assessment and list suggestions for improvement. A five-point scale is used to determine compliance with a standard or guideline. The range of ratings is one (indicating that the standard is "not met") through five (indicating that the standard is "fully met"). Ratings of INA and EX indicate either "Information Not Available" (INA) or that the program rates "Exemplary" (EX). When totaling the scores in a section, INA translates to one and EX translates to five. INAs can be particularly helpful indicators; and while you know that you are performing at a certain level, it may not be obvious to others. You then have an opportunity to create the appropriate documentation for your unit.

Implementing Change

Organization of the process is imperative. As you may have already recognized, there is a lot of program material to review and rate. The CAS process indicates that each reviewer should rate each of the standards and guidelines individually and then gather as a group to compare and discuss any discrepancies in the ratings. After consensus is reached, the assessment team, in consultation with the staff or other appropriate individuals, should review the results of the assessment and provide suggestions for improvement in the areas that were not fully met. An action plan should be developed that includes the areas in which the unit excelled, the required changes to meet standards, and suggestions for enhancing the unit. Suggestions and required changes should be prioritized; and a timeline, individuals responsible for implementation, and the resources required to implement them should be clearly identified.

Benefits and Challenges

The CAS process offers a number of benefits. By participating in the process and implementing change based on the results, programs may increase credibility. Programs that participate are able to demonstrate that the program is consistent with national standards and then have internal benchmarks for future assessment. The CAS standards and guidelines can be used to assist with the development of new programs or restructuring of existing programs. They may also be used to provide professional development of staff (Miller, 1999). Most importantly, with the inclusion of the learning and development outcomes to the program standards, units can measure the impact of their program on students' growth. They not only provide evidence that their program contributes to student learning and development, but also use the information gathered for continuous improvement as discussed in Chapter Two.

The most significant challenges to the process are finding team members willing to spend the time on the process and finding time to prepare materials for the review. While these are challenges, they can be overcome. Ways to address each can be found in strategies to manage resources, data, and documentation.

Strategies to Manage Resources, Data, and Documentation

Assessment can feel overwhelming, and the CAS process is no exception. It is easy to assume that managing the CAS process will be easy because others will be reading the lengthy materials, providing ratings, and making suggestions for improvement. In addition to these critical pieces of the process, there are other important tasks that must be completed. If you choose to participate in a CAS self-study, you would need to ensure that you provide the review team with well-organized materials for the review. If you do not provide them with well-organized documentation, it will be almost impossible for the team to conduct a thorough review. Gathering and organizing all the documentation is far more complicated than one might expect; therefore, allowing plenty of time for the task is critical. For example, you might want to consider devoting one semester to reviewing each standard and guideline as if you were the reviewer. You are likely to find that some of your practices are not documented in writing. This may be true of the standards as well as student learning and development outcomes in the "program" section. This may require creating new office manuals (or sections of manuals) or providing other types of documentation such as e-mails or letters that demonstrate how you meet certain standards. This process will take time and can be very tedious. We suggest you plan on devoting time to this so that you get the most out of the time the reviewers spend with your documentation. Once the review is completed, you will also participate in the review of the results and the creation of the action plan.

Another way to manage this process is to reduce its size. There are several ways you can accomplish this task. In the frequently asked questions section of the CAS website, they remind you that it is not required to use all the standards at one time. You may decide to only review some portion of the standards (Miller, 1999). To better manage the process, you could review the standards during the first assessment phase (e.g., first academic year) and, if you like, review the guidelines during another assessment phase.

Another way to manage the project is to restructure how the review is conducted. While certainly the idea of all reviewers seeing all the documentation and discussing it is the most thorough way to conduct the process, it may be difficult to find staff and faculty able to devote that level of involvement. You might consider having more reviewers and then creating teams of two to review only specified sections of the SAG (Table 6–1).

TABLE 6–1

Cost-savings Tips

The cost of the SAG for a particular unit can be very inexpensive (see www.cas.edu). The most significant cost is printing. If you provide copies to all three to five reviewers of all the documentation for the 13 sections, your costs may be quite high. Using a modified version of the implementation, such as dividing the reviewers into teams to review only some sections or only have the team review selected sections each year, will reduce cost. Another option is to put the documentation online. If you have a staff member that has web capabilities, you could devote a section of your program's website to the process. For example, a page per section with links to the various documents would be a simple way to provide what is needed to the reviewers.

Involving Students

There are several ways to incorporate students into the CAS process. One obvious way to involve students is to include one or more on your review team. You may choose to include students that have had contact with your office and are familiar with your program, or you may want to include students that have little knowledge of your office or program so that you can ensure that your documentation is speaking for itself.

Another option is to include students in the preparation of the CAS documentation. Students that have extensive experience with your office may be able to assist with pulling documentation together, and in some cases actually creating documents that have not existed in the past. Involving a student in this manner would be a wonderful way to test their knowledge of the work and intention of your unit.

The CAS process is an excellent way to review your program and to move you toward determining how your program is impacting student learning. The aforementioned information was designed to provide you with basic instructions about the process, but we highly recommend visiting the CAS website at http://www.cas.edu to read more about how engaging in a review can assist with continuous improvement of your unit.

CHAPTER 7

Best Practices, Performance Indicators, Benchmarking, Peer Reviews, and External Reviews

---

This chapter will be a bit different from the others in that we will be focusing on the considerations for using best practices, performance indicators, benchmarking, peer reviews, and external reviews to assess any student learning and development outcome, rather than discussing whether it is the appropriate choice for your particular outcome. The purpose of such an illustration is not to discourage you from using best practices, performance indicators, benchmarking, peer reviews, and external reviews to evaluate student learning. Rather, we desire to present issues to consider prior to your use of these methods.

What is Benchmarking?

Spendolini (1992) defines benchmarking as a "continuous systematic process for evaluating the products, services, and work processes of organizations that are recognized as representing best practices for the purposes of organizational improvement" (p. 9). You can see by this definition and the definition of assessment posed in Chapter Two that there are similarities behind the purpose of benchmarking and the purpose of assessment. Both benchmarking and assessment are about improvement, and both definitions stress the importance of a systematic process in order to evaluate. While assessment and benchmarking both focus on "products, services, and work processes;" benchmarking highlights a comparative evaluation of products, services, and work processes based on best practices or to establish best practices. The assessment process described in Chapter Two may not necessarily be concerned about comparing its products, services, and work processes with that of another unit's, be it inside the institution, outside the institution, or outside of higher education; however, you can certainly choose to use comparative methods in your assessment plan.

What are the Implications for Using Benchmarking to Assess Student Learning and Development?

The primary point of comparing the definition of benchmarking to the definition of assessment is to explain that when you are using benchmarking in your assessment plan, you are committing yourself to comparing your results with other best practices, be they inside your institution, outside your institution, or outside of higher education (The Benchmarking Exchange, 2003). The reason we make this point so strong is not to ask you to declare a value judgment as to whether this kind of comparison is good or bad (indeed, we find benchmarking extremely valuable for many of our services and processes and, thus, use it whenever we are able), but to make note of it in your assessment planning. For, when you benchmark, you are typically choosing to make the results of your findings public. That is a primary purpose of benchmarking (Ewell, 1997b; Upcraft & Schuh, 1996).

While we highly encourage transparency in assessment (Allen & Bresciani, 2003), we also recognize that organizationally it may be detrimental for some institutions, particularly if you are just beginning with implementing systematic assessment. Furthermore, if you choose to benchmark, benchmarking services and processes sometimes may feel a little less vulnerable than benchmarking a "product" such as student learning and development.

While we recognize that benchmarking student learning and development is extremely controversial and should be approached with great care and attentiveness, we do not want to end here with the question of whether it should or should not be done. That is for you to decide. The purpose of this chapter is to illustrate considerations for you when making your own decision about benchmarking your student learning and development outcomes.

Through all this, keep in mind that one of the most valuable attributes of benchmarking is that it allows you to "stop, and look up" from your program and examine how well you are comparing with others. Benchmarking is intended, as the definition describes, to provide an opportunity to learn about what you can improve through the systematic comparison of the outcomes of your products, services, and work processes (The Benchmarking Project, 2003; Upcraft & Schuh, 1996). In order to do this well, there are a number of deliberations to be made before embarking on a benchmarking project.

Considerations for Using Benchmarking to Assess Student Learning and Development

- Is your organization ready to share publicly the evidence you have for meeting student learning and development outcomes? You do not always have to share your information publicly. Some benchmarking projects allow you to share your information within a group of similar institutions, thus your institution's information may not be as identifiable. However, when using benchmarking, you may want to be ready to share your information publicly as the comparability of the student learning typically requires institutions to explain the intricacies of who they are in order to make the information more meaningful, especially for decisions of continuous improvement.

- Would it be valuable for you to benchmark the services and processes that contribute to the student learning and development outcomes prior to benchmarking your student learning and development evidence?

- Prior to benchmarking, have you educated your constituents about what benchmarking means and how the information is used to make decisions for improvement?

- Do you have access to the tools that will help you benchmark responsibly? For example, the National Survey of Student Engagement (Center for Postsecondary Research & Planning, Indiana University, 2003), College and University Counseling Center Directors Data Bank (The Benchmarking Exchange, 2003), Educational Benchmarking Incorporated surveys (2003), American College Health Association Survey (2003), National Association of Colleges and Employers Career Services surveys (1998), the National Survey of Counseling Center Directors (The Benchmarking Exchange, 2003) surveys, and others (see Chapter Twelve for more information on surveys).

- Have you already discussed the various scenarios among your key administrators about how you plan to use the information and how they may be able to assist you?

- Will the evidence that you are using to evaluate whether you have met your learning outcome be "benchmarkable?" In other words, if you want to compare the evidence to demonstrate your students have learned how to think critically with another program's students or another institution' students, what evidence are you presenting for comparison? Will that other institution have the same evidence? Often, benchmarking efforts fall apart because we are not comparing similar types of "data" and, thus, the results or the interpretation of the results cannot be compared.

- Which institutions allow you to compare yourself in a meaningful manner? While you may be very impressed with the best practices of a private liberal arts college's first-year program, the public Research I university that you are at may not make the best comparison. Once more, many community colleges can make decisions and changes for improvement faster and thus may be on the "cutting edge" of assessment, while other institutional types have to wade through their organizational bureaucracies. Similarly, keep in mind institutional culture. We have seen challenges in comparing spiritual learning and development outcomes at similar types of institutions just because one was influenced by the culture of the south and the other by the culture of the northeast.

After addressing these considerations and deciding that benchmarking is still a good idea, consider the steps listed in Table 7-1 to implement benchmarking.

TABLE 7–1

Steps in the Benchmarking Process
(Source: Adapted from Upcraft & Schuh, 1996.)

1) Define the outcome you want benchmarked.

2) Make sure benchmarking is appropriate. This is also a great place to state whether or not you just want a comparative benchmark or a best practices benchmark. Just conducting a benchmark does not mean you will have a best practices comparison.

3) Determine the following: What will you benchmark? What is the evidence that will help you understand the learning and development outcome? How will you gather it and analyze it? How will you report it?

4) Choose who should be involved in the benchmarking project.

5) Select comparable organizations to benchmark against — either from within the institution, from another institution, or from outside higher education.

6) Determine funding for the benchmarking project.

7) Ensure that all constituents are properly educated about the value and use of benchmarking.

8) Discuss scenarios of potential results with key decision-makers.

9) Submit data to organization conducting the benchmark.

10) Get results back, interpret them, and make decision and recommendations.

11) Strategically disseminate findings and an action plan for improvement.

Providing opportunities for comparison is extremely valuable, especially when best practices are used. If benchmarking appears too overwhelming, especially since we are focusing on benchmarking of student learning and development, consider other alternatives.

Example of a Model for Learning and Assessment Being Used for Benchmarking
Linking Strategic Learning to Indicators of Progress: The Valencia Community College Model
The unique challenges that confront many community colleges (CCs) have often hindered the development of policies, processes, and structures that would support a "learning-centered" institutional philosophy. Although pockets of effectiveness and excellence exist at many of these campuses, what is needed is a comprehensive

commitment to institutional effectiveness and continuous improvement. Several CCs have committed to redesigning themselves as "learning-centered" institutions as they simultaneously commit to an institutional model of assessment (e.g., Maricopa CC, Isothermal CC, Takoma CC, Valencia CC).

The Valencia CC Model
Starting in 1995, Valencia CC moved through a three-phase process that led to the development and implementation of a Strategic Learning Plan. The process was a deliberate attempt to institutionalize effective innovations and to focus on improving measurable outcomes.

- Phase I (1995–1998) was focused on encouraging dialogue and building consensus throughout the college for becoming a more learning-centered institution.

- Phase II (1998–2000) was marked by intentional efforts to move the initiative from talk to action. Substantive changes were evident in areas like administrative support of the learning process and in the development of new student core competencies.

- Phase III (2000–2004) was the point of convergence of all the preceding work. This phase saw the college articulate clear statements of institutional purpose and develop and begin to implement seven new strategic learning goals through collaborative college-wide planning meetings, work groups, action teams, and governing council recommendations.

Intentionality of Implementation
Valencia's seven strategic goals were developed with enhanced student learning as the central driving force. Moreover, the institution has made a public commitment to emphasize the intentional component of the collaborative process that created the plan by developing outcomes, strategies, and action agenda items for each goal. Other aspects of intentionality include:

- Each action item related to a goal has an individual assigned to lead the action, a governing council responsible for oversight of the activity, and a deadline for the completion of the activity.

- Assessment data that is generated will be gauged relative to Indicators of Progress that have been identified and approved.

<u>Supporting Learning Leaders</u>

One unique aspect of the Valencia CC model of learning and assessment is the emphasis that is placed on the empowered professional development of faculty and staff who are identified as learning leaders throughout the organization. While this is often alluded to in other models, it generally is not addressed directly. Valencia CC seeks to accomplish this goal by incorporating the following strategies:

- Create a new recruitment, hiring, induction, and support model for all faculty and staff that reflects learning-centered principles and the value of diversity to learning.

- Increase faculty engagement of students by improving the ratio of full-time career faculty to adjunct and four-month faculty, especially in foundation courses.

- Review and revise performance feedback processes to reflect learning-centered principles and results.

- Review and redesign college and campus programs for continual professional development, revitalization, and recognition of all faculty and staff to reflect learning-centered principles.

- Review and revise the College's compensation systems to reflect learning-centered principles.

- Revise the college's organizational structure—including senior management, departments, and learning support—to reflect learning-centered principles; foster leadership at all levels of the organization.

- Support faculty innovation in curriculum, teaching, instructional support, and assessment, especially in foundation courses.

The Valencia CC model of learning and assessment could serve as a benchmark for two- and four-year institutions due to sound conceptualization, intentional commitment to learning, attention to professional development, and a comprehensive approach to outcomes assessment and continuous improvement.

Peer Review

An alternative to benchmarking is peer review (Ewell, 1997). The peer review process allows for the unit to articulate what they find most valuable in regards to student learning and development and then have that unit's findings reviewed by a set of specially selected peers. The peers (individual cocurricular specialists) can compare what they find at your program with what they have found at other programs. They also can examine your learning outcomes against a set of predefined best practices. For example, you could ask a set of peers to evaluate the assessment results from the learning outcomes of your living learning community against either a set of your peer institution's living learning communities or the nation's Living Learning Community identified Best Practice sites.

Using the aforementioned method, you may get a comparative analysis. But if done well, you get an evaluation against certain standards and expectations that will help you personally identify your best practice shortcomings, and you may receive assistance as to what can be improved. Ewell's (1997a) advice for a quality peer review process includes "a meaningful academically owned, nongovernmental approach to quality assurance" (p. 18). The aforementioned method seems to fit Ewell's description well.

Peer reviews can also consist of selecting institutions that have programs or outcomes similar to yours and then electronically exchanging information with those peers about your learning outcomes, analysis, and resulting decisions (The Integrated Postsecondary Education Data System [IPEDS], 2003). While this method is usually more cost-effective than inviting (and paying for external) peers to visit your campus, it becomes a little more challenging for exactly the same reasons that were articulated in regards to implementing benchmarking. In other words, it is often difficult to exchange similar data and interpretations of that data (Ewell, 1997a). Both the challenges and implementation processes of data exchanges between peer institutions and benchmarking are similar.

External Review

Another way to evaluate the results of your learning and development outcomes is to invite an external review (Palomba & Banta, 1999). An external review is much like what was described in the peer review, except that it can be conducted on or off-site. In other words, if you would like to have a cocurricular specialist evaluate your academic advising program portfolio (e.g., the student learning and development outcomes, evidence, results, and decisions you made), it may be possible for you to just send the reviewer all that information. Then, if necessary, the reviewer can visit the campus to "take a closer look." If not, the evaluation is done in a more cost-effective manner.

Up to this point, we have primarily been discussing the use of peer reviews, external reviews, and to some extent even benchmarking as an evaluation of what you have learned about what your students are learning and how they are developing. These methods indeed are very rich for such use. And in order for these methods to remain of value, they should supplement the assessment work that you are already doing. In other words, your assessment plan should not just consist of peer reviews, external reviews, or benchmarking.

In order for systematic ongoing assessment to take hold and have meaning, those delivering the programs that contribute to student learning and development must implement the outcomes and the assessment process to evaluate them. If not, assessment will always be perceived as an add-on project or as a "grade" for how well an outcome has been achieved, rather than as the improvement process that it is. It is one thing to invite an external reviewer or a team of peers to check on how well you are doing in the assessment of your outcomes and to offer their recommendations. It is quite another for them to be your sole source of evaluation of the outcome.

With all this conversation about who should be doing the evaluating of the student learning and development outcomes, we have been ignoring the multiple references to the criteria used for evaluation. In Chapter Five, we discussed criteria and rubrics. Here we will use the same principles learned in Chapter Five and apply them to words we often hear in this context, best practices, and performance indicators.

Best Practices

Best practices are often referred to in benchmarking (Upcraft & Schuh, 1996). Best practices are typically the finest examples of process, program delivery, or methods in a given area that produce the highest known quality outcomes (Palomba & Banta, 1999). Best practices are usually determined by those meeting and exceeding a list of criteria (although not always). So, in some cases a list of criteria may make up a best practice. In another case, an example of high performance of a specific list of criteria may constitute a best practice. The end result is that by being named a best practice, a new set of criteria or standards is created in which to aspire. Best practices are sometimes referred to as performance indicators, because they can represent measures as well as criteria depending on how they are used (The Benchmarking Project, 2003).

Sometimes, people call best practices "benchmarks;" others may call them "standards." Again, various definitions are used in various settings, so be sure that if you choose to use any of these terms, you define them for your use on your campus.

Performance Indicators

If you have ever worked in enrollment management, you have heard the term "performance indicators" more times than you want to count. Similar to many of the terms discussed in this book, performance indicators mean different things to different people. Performance indicators can denote the list of measures used by *U.S. World and News Report* to rank institutions. Thus, retention rates, graduation rates, and incoming average SAT scores make up performance indicators. To make it even more confusing, you can set a benchmark for an 85 percent first-year retention rate, and that can be referred to as a performance indicator or a benchmark, depending on to whom you are speaking.

Ewell (1997b) states that the primary value of performance indicators is their comparative purpose. Because of the rules set forth by IPEDS, it is very easy to compare retention rates and six-year graduation rates from one campus to the other. Cumulative grade point averages (GPAs), while less systematic from institution to institution, can still be called a performance indicator and used for comparative purposes.

Ewell (1997b) further defines an indicator as a "relevant, easily calculable statistic that reflects the overall condition of an enterprise" (p. 609). There are two primary pieces of information in this quote. One is that a performance indicator is easily calculable; and if used for comparison purposes, that means easily calculable across institutions. In regards to assessing student learning and development across institutional types, and across divisions and disciplines, there are many measures that are not "easily calculable across institutions."

Before getting discouraged, note that Ewell further discusses that an indicator must be relevant. Few of the indicators in wide use today are relevant to assessing student learning and development. If you take the list of student learning and development outcomes for your program (e.g., communication, creative thinking, decision making, problem solving, reasoning, cultural awareness, analyzing information, personal responsibility, wellness, conflict resolution), very few (note we did not say NONE) can be evaluated by performance indicators such as retention rates, graduation rates, and faculty-to-student ratio. Now, if you take the wealth of research we know about class-size and student engagement and the positive impact these types of experiences have on learning, then we can begin to make sense out of these performance indicators. Yet, if we use them in isolation, how would we know what to improve?

For example, let's say you have an outcome that, *students attending 12 activities in the fine arts series will have retention rates greater than those who do not attend*. The analysis is a comparative retention analysis, attempting to control for all other factors that influence retention. Your result is that you discover this cohort of students does have a higher retention rate. Congratulations. What are you going to do with your program; keep it the same? Okay, what have your students learned and how have they developed? Hmm. Furthermore, if the retention outcome is the only outcome you had, then you do not know how your program contributed to increased retention. If you were assessing other outcomes along with it, such as student learning and development types of outcomes, then you can continue to improve your program and inform administrators in more detail as to why your program is contributing to increased retention rates. This is especially valuable for the years that students in your program do not have higher retention rates.

The point of this illustration is to emphasize that while many performance indicators may not appear relevant, they can become relevant if you do the type of meaningful assessment that supports your performance indicator findings. As Ewell states (1997b), performance indicators are exactly that—they are proxies of an institution's or program's condition. They in no way inform anyone as to the cause of the value found in the indicator, nor do they provide any indication of how to improve. So, feel free to use performance indicators as measures of your programs, but be sure to incorporate those other extremely valuable student learning and development outcomes so that you can explain what you are finding.

TABLE 7–2

Cost-saving Tips

- Invite internal peer reviewers.
- Invite undergraduate and graduate students to conduct performance indicator research on your program. They can capture and crunch the data while you assess the learning and development outcomes.
- Invite faculty in public policy to assist with reviews.

CHAPTER 8

Interviews and Focus Groups

Individual interviews and focus group interviews are two of the more commonly used qualitative methods in assessment. It is not uncommon to hear cocurricular professionals say that they will conduct "interviews and focus groups" when describing their assessment work. While there may be some clear distinctions in procedures between interviewing individuals and conducting focus group interviews, they are often mentioned together. Due to this tendency, we chose to present them to you jointly, knowing that there is more than enough information concerning each method to warrant separate chapters. We made this decision so that you can compare and contrast, thus making the best decision possible regarding which method you might apply. There may be times when you choose one type of interview over another, and times when you decide to do both. For simplicity, individual interviews will be referred to as "interviews" and focus group interviews will be referred to as "focus groups."

Description

There are many ways to conduct interviews and focus groups. So, to be sure that a basic understanding exists, a very brief description of each follows.

According to Maykut and Morehouse (1994), an interview is a purposeful discussion. Bogdan and Biklen (1998, p. 93) add that interviews are "directed by one in order to get information form the other." Interviews vary in level of structure and last approximately thirty minutes to an hour (Bogdan & Biklen, 1998), and there are usually predetermined questions or topics that determine what is discussed during the interview (Patton, 2002).

According to Patton (2002, p. 385), focus groups are described as "an interview with a small group of people on a specific topic." Patton suggests that focus groups consist of six to ten people, and Krueger (1994) suggests that there be one facilitator and one note taker. According to Patton (2002), focus groups usually require one to two hours to facilitate. A list of questions or topics is used to lead the group as they discuss the topics. The participants interact with the facilitator and the other subjects providing answers to the questions. The facilitator is usually free to make adjustments to the list and ask follow-up questions as appropriate.

Why Use Interviews and Focus Groups?

There are a number of reasons to use interviews and focus groups for assessment in the cocurricular, but the most obvious and significant benefit is that interviews and focus groups are excellent methods of gathering rich detail (Marshall & Rossman, 1999). While interviewers and focus group facilitators have a list of questions or topics that they use during the session, in less structured settings they are free to stray from the list whenever necessary (Patton, 2002). This offers the opportunity to gather deeper levels of information, which is valuable when assessing learning. For example, realizing that students did not learn what you wanted them to learn is not enough for meaningful improvement. If possible, knowing why they did not learn the information and investigating ways in which they would have better understood the material would provide the level of detail needed to make meaningful improvement.

The rich information gathered during interviews and focus groups can be useful in many ways. Due to the ability to seek immediate clarification and context (Marshall & Rossman, 1999), interviews and focus groups offer an opportunity to gather data on subjects that we know little about. This option is particularly attractive because it is very difficult to write meaningful survey questions about subjects for which there is little information.

Interviews and focus groups can also be used to learn more about survey data. For example, if the results of a survey indicate that students did not learn what was expected, interviews and focus groups could be conducted to assist in determining where the breakdown occurred and ways to improve the learning process. Regardless of the specificity of a survey, interviews and focus groups are both excellent ways for following up on important data.

Example Outcomes
The following statements are examples of outcomes for which interviews and focus groups might be useful methods of gathering data. The three examples below are very different types of outcomes but may all be part of a training program for resident assistants (RA) in a housing setting. In this case, RAs attend a weeklong training where there are one-hour sessions on topics that are believed to be necessary for them to be successful in their positions. These outcomes will be used throughout this chapter to demonstrate issues to consider as methods are chosen, tools are developed, implementation is designed and carried out, and data are interpreted and used for improvement:

- Students will demonstrate knowledge of the available campus resources.

- Students will demonstrate effective and appropriate confrontation skills.

- Students will demonstrate effective time management.

- Students will articulate "the impact of diversity on one's own society" (Miller, 1999, p. 19).

These outcomes suggest that it is an expectation that the student staff learned and developed as part of the preparation to be an RA. But how will we know that they can do what we have stated above? Interviews or focus groups, possibly in addition to other forms of measurement, may help determine our effectiveness and how to improve when appropriate.

Interviews and focus groups can be used to supplement other methods of data collection. In addition to supporting the creation of surveys and gathering follow-up data, interviews and focus groups may be used to supplement

observations, document analysis, the CAS process, case studies, and portfolios. For the example outcomes mentioned above, interviews and focus groups would allow the person conducting the assessment to ask questions that would provide information about knowledge gained (campus resources and impact of diversity on one's own society) and behavior (application of learning time management and confrontation skills). In addition, through either planned questions or spontaneous follow-up questions, they would allow the assessor to learn about the process that did, or in some cases did not, lead to the learning and development. Both methods will allow the practitioner to gather the type of data necessary to make meaningful improvement, but are both interviews and focus groups equally appropriate or necessary for measuring these outcomes?

Interviews, Focus Groups, or Both?
Choosing to do interviews and focus groups may be an easy decision; but choosing between the two, if required, may be more difficult. While both methods seem to be appropriate to measure the examples thus far, there are other issues to consider that may cause us to choose one over the other. With the notion of assessment needing to be manageable, doing both may not be reasonable. In addition, reflection on the topic, time frame, population, level of available assistance, budget, and fit into the regular assessment cycle may cause us to consider one method over the other.

Topic
When determining whether interviews or focus groups are appropriate methods, consider the nature of the topic to be addressed. Is the issue to be discussed extremely sensitive or volatile? Is it the type of topic that some students may feel uncomfortable responding to in front of other students? If so, individual interviews may provide a sense of security for the participant. Discussing topics that are sensitive or volatile in a group setting may be uncomfortable, and students may not provide you with truthful responses. If the topic is not sensitive or volatile, focus groups may provide an opportunity for students to hear others' views and, thus, provide more thoughtful answers.

In the examples provided, the topics do not appear to be excessively threatening. Some RAs may feel less comfortable discussing the diversity issues in a group setting. One strategy to assist in determining the usefulness of a focus group is to reflect on the RA training session or sessions that provided the information. Were the students able to share in the session? Did it appear to be a safe environment? If the students did not participate or the session took a negative tone, you might decide that individual interviews may be more productive. If the sessions appeared to go well and students appeared comfortable with the topic, then focus groups might be the best choice.

Time Frame

Another consideration when choosing between interviews and focus groups is time frame. If your time is limited, focus groups will allow you to gather information from a larger number of students in less time. Of course the assumption in this scenario is that students attend the focus group. Setting up focus groups and ensuring attendance is no easy task. Some may argue that individual interviews are faster and easier because they are scheduled based on individuals' calendars and the one-on-one request to talk may be taken more seriously, so students may be more likely to attend.

Time frame may be a concern in the RA training example. If the RAs are not learning and developing as stated in the learning and development outcomes, then they may not be effective staff in the residence halls, and this has a direct impact on the students that live there. It would be important to determine if these outcomes were met in a timely manner so that the results could benefit the current staff and ultimately the other students. For example, the assessment of the outcome "Students will demonstrate knowledge of the available campus resources" should occur early in the first semester so that if the learning and development did not occur, decisions for improvements can be made. The decisions may include retraining of some staff and changes to the original training for the following year.

Size of the Population

If you have a large population and want to gather information from a larger number of students, focus groups may again be a good alternative. It is important to note that interviews and focus groups are not designed to be statistically representative samples of entire populations, but rather to gather rich detailed information from participants chosen purposefully (Glesne, 1999). However, it is important to get representative points of view. If the population is large, hour for hour, you will likely reach more students using focus groups than individual interviews. The population in the RA training example is the RA staff of approximately 150. The

size of the group is relatively small so individual interviews or focus groups would be appropriate.

Assistance

Another issue to consider is whether you will have help conducting your assessment. It is beneficial to have another person assist with focus groups. While taping the focus group is also recommended, having a note taker is important. In individual interviews, the interviewer is able to take notes and conduct the interview. Focus groups are much more complex, and it is very difficult to take meaningful notes and facilitate a conversation among six to eight students.

Budget

It is suggested that interviews and focus groups be taped; thus, a tape recorder, tapes, and transcription of these tapes will be needed for both. As previously mentioned, focus groups will require fewer tapes per student than interviews. The next financial issue to consider is the cost of transcripts. It is efficient to have tapes transcribed by a third party, but that is very costly. Transcribing the tapes yourself is obviously free but very time consuming and tedious. Due to the complex nature of a focus group conversation, both the cost to have tapes transcribed and the length of time to do it yourself are increased.

Another cost-related matter to consider is offering incentives. Incentives such as free food, cash, or entries into drawings help attract students to interviews and focus groups. If you have a limited amount of funding, pizza and drinks may help draw students to the group; but if you have the budget, drawings for gift certificates to the bookstore or other prizes may be more effective.

How Easily Can I Fit This Method Into My Responsibilities on a Regular Basis?

The practitioner should define the term "regular." Some assessment needs to occur daily, some monthly, some yearly, and so on. You make that decision. Regardless of the choice to do interviews, focus groups, or both, consider how often they should occur for the most meaningful improvement and find a way to incorporate them into your regular responsibilities. Individual interviews conducted regularly may be easier to accommodate. They may become exit interviews or pre-involvement interviews. In the RA training example, focus group methodology may be used as part of a monthly staff meeting to gain information on training effectiveness for resident advisors. After the staff meeting is over or in place of a staff meeting, the trainer could talk to the group of RAs about subjects from the learning and development outcomes. The trainer could ask questions that either required the RAs to demonstrate the actual learning or development, such as asking them to respond to case studies or to self-report learning and development in regards to the outcomes.

You Can Always Do Both!

This chapter was not designed to make you feel as if you had to choose either interviews or focus groups. If you have the resources to do both, that is fabulous. The more methods used to gather data, the stronger your assessment and thus the more useful the information (Maki, 2001).

Basic Implementation Tips

There are many wonderful resources with detailed information regarding implementation of interview and focus group methodology. It is not possible to cover all the material that we would like to cover in this text. We have included the basics of what you should consider and some of the options available to you, but you should consider reviewing some of the references and additional resources listed at the end of the book. For the purposes of this text, we will discuss sample, protocols, interviewer and moderator preparation, strategies for successful moderating, note taking, and data analysis.

Sample: Who Do I Invite To Participate?

Qualitative research methods such as focus groups and interviews are not designed to have statistically representative samples. Instead, the samples are chosen based upon the nature of the study. Patton (2002, p. 230) says "What would be 'bias' in statistical sampling, and therefore a weakness, becomes intended focus in qualitative sampling, and therefore a strength. The logic and power of purposeful sampling lie in selecting information-rich cases for study in-depth." Glesne (1999) suggests considering the variables most important in your study and including those in the sample; but he advises that you not "get overinvested in including all the possible configurations of such variables" and to remember that "the selection strategy is often refined" (pp. 29–30) as the study develops. For example, the sample for the RA training assessment would not need to be a perfect representation of the entire RA population at the university. On the other hand, we would not want to only interview women RAs or RAs of only one race or from one

staff. We would still attempt to gather views across gender, race, and work settings.

There are a number of ways to choose samples and a common method used in interviews and focus groups is purposeful sampling. Purposeful sampling involves choosing subjects that you believe will be able to provide you with important information (Patton, 2002; Bogdan & Biklen, 1998). One type of purposeful sample described by Patton (2002) is "stratified." Stratified means purposefully choosing participants from various sub-groups. In the RA training example, you would want to choose your sample from all RAs that attended training. If the RA staff structure is such that there are five areas of campus and each area has six staffs, you may choose to stratify by conducting a focus group with at least one staff per section of campus. That would give you five focus groups insuring that each of the areas of campus is represented. You could then review the demographics of each staff to ensure that the group is diverse. The same idea applies for choosing interview participants.

Other types of purposeful sampling include "maximum variation," "typical case," "critical case," and "extreme or deviant case" (Patton, 1989, pp. 100–107). For more information on purposeful sampling, please review the references and additional resources listed at the end of the book. Patton's (2002) new version of *Qualitative Research and Evaluation Methods* provides wonderful information on sampling.

Another way to choose a sample is by using key informants. A key informant is a specific person that you believe will give you the most information about the subject you are assessing (LeCompte & Pressle, 1993; Patton, 2002). Key informants are sometimes used to help test or develop interview and focus group protocols. Other times they are used to begin snowball sampling. If you were assessing the factors that contributed to a problem with the retention of RAs, you may ask an RA that you know well and that you believe will trust you and honestly answer your questions to be the first person interviewed. This key information may help you identify some of the issues you should be researching as well as suggest who to contact next.

Snowball sampling (Glesne, 1999; LeCompte & Preissle, 1993; Patton, 2002) is used when the population you are aiming to assess is hidden or unknown. The population may be hidden because the topic is threatening, such as talking to students about the cheating behaviors they see on campus, or it may be that you are unsure who has information about what you are assessing (Glesne, 1999). You start with a key informant or someone that you know has information about the topic; then once your interview is over, you ask the participant to provide you with names of those that will be able to provide you with more information. This process is not likely to work with focus groups.

Convenience sampling (Patton, 2002) is exactly as it sounds. Essentially, convenience sampling is when interviewees are chosen based on availability alone. For example, if you want to know about the impact of an RA training session that was campus wide and you only interview the RAs that work for you, you are not likely to get a variety of views. While it is easy and cost effective, it is best to avoid this if at all possible. According to Patton (2002), it leads to "information-poor" (p. 244) subjects and, not so surprisingly, less credibility in the study.

Sample: How Many Is Enough?

The issue of sample size in qualitative methodologies is one that raises many questions. Those engaged in assessment are usually interested in doing quality work; and when doing interviews and focus groups, the size of the sample is often a concern for the assessor. As mentioned previously, the purpose is not to have a statistically significant sample. Patton (2002, p. 244) says,

> There are no rules for sample size in qualitative inquiry. Sample size depends on what you want to know, the purpose of the inquiry, what's at stake, what will be useful, what will have credibility, and what can be done with available time and resources.

This is difficult for some to comprehend. Quantitative methods have rules regarding sample size, so it is not uncommon for those engaging in qualitative methods to look for guidance on this issue. It is very easy to be engaged in interviewing or conducting focus groups and suddenly feel as if you are not doing quality research because you are thinking about the quantitative rules. It is very important to remember that qualitative and quantitative methodologies are different.

When determining sample size for interviews and focus groups, there are several issues to consider that are embedded in Patton's previous statement, but worth mentioning separately. Something to note is that Patton does mention credibility in his list of issues to consider. Ensuring that you have done everything you can to get

the variation in sample that is reflective of the population will help the credibility of your study (Seidman, 1998).

Another importation consideration when determining if your sample is large enough is the notion of saturation (Lincoln & Guba, 1985). Saturation refers to the point at which you feel that you are hearing the same responses over and over and nothing new is emerging. Of course, you do not want to stop your inquiry the first time you hear something twice or even three times. Balance is required when making this judgment.

Knowing why you chose to stop gathering data, whether because you did not have the budget to continue or you reached saturation, and communicating that in your documentation is imperative. In remaining credible to your constituents, providing such explanations helps them understand that you did not stop the sample because you haphazardly decided you had enough information. There were reasons for your decisions, and those reasons are supported by the literature on qualitative methodology.

Sample: Other Considerations

Once you have chosen your sampling methods there are other issues to consider: How will you invite your participants? If it is a focus group, will you advertise the group and see who shows up, or will you ask specific people to attend? For interviews and focus groups with invited participants, will you send letters, ask in person, or make phone calls? Will you then do reminders just prior to the group or interview? Will you have incentives? If so, where will that funding come from (e.g., grants, donations)? As with any important project there are always lots of detail items to consider. Plan for those as much as you can. There will always be little unexpected items that arise throughout the project.

Interview and Focus Group Protocols: Level of Structure

Determining the level of structure you want to have during an interview is necessary so that you are able to make decisions about changes to the interview protocol as new topics arise. Interviews can be unstructured, semi-structured, or structured (Patton, 2002). Patton refers to interviews that are unstructured as informal conversations. Much as you would expect in an informal conversation, there are rarely any predetermined questions and the interview may cover a number of topics and not be consistent with the next informal interview. Often, the interviews build upon what was learned in earlier interviews, allowing the interviewer to explore topics of interest.

Interviews that are semi-structured are referred to by Patton (2002) as guided interviews. In guided interviews, the interviewer has prepared a list of topics to cover during the interview, thus ensuring that there is consistency. This style of delivery allows the flow of the conversation to develop more naturally, and the interviewer is freer to explore unclear responses and new ideas as needed. This level of structure also allows the interviewer to phrase the questions in a way that matches the flow and feel of the conversation. This type of guide provides the necessary structure to ensure that all topics are covered, yet allows the interviewer to develop rapport with the interviewee and to follow the natural flow of the conversation.

Semi-structured protocols may be an appropriate choice for focus groups. When you consider that one of the benefits of focus groups is that students are responding to each other, therefore providing even more rich detail, it would be very difficult not to have a less structured format.

Patton (2002) refers to the most structured type of interview as "the standardized open-ended interview." In this case, interview protocols are highly structured, including the opening remarks. If it is necessary to set the stage prior to asking a question, those remarks are standardized as well. For some, this type of interview has more credibility. It is proof that every student is asked the same question in the same way, and often the wording of each question is approved by external constituents prior to any interviews. The limitation is that follow-up on unexpected responses is not possible.

According to Patton (2002), you do not have to choose one approach. It may be more appropriate to combine the approaches. In the RA training example, you may need to ask more structured questions if you desire direct evidence of learning on certain outcomes. The questions may be very carefully worded in an attempt to elicit specific ideas taught during training. This will allow for better analysis using a very specific set of criteria (see Chapter Five). Other questions may be based on a list of topics to cover and worded as the conversation evolves. For example, to get at information regarding time management, you may talk with them about their RA position and the balance with full-time student status. The question may seem less formal and flow nicely with the conversation, but you still receive

the information you need to determine if they are able to apply the time management skills taught in class to their life.

Protocol Questions

Direct and Indirect Evidence
Interviews and focus groups can be used to gather direct or indirect evidence of learning and development. One of the example outcomes for RA training is "Students will demonstrate knowledge of the available campus resources." During the interview, the student could be asked to list a specified number of campus resources. If the student can provide the information that the interview expects them to know, that is direct evidence. Asking them if they know the resources available and them replying that they do is self-report and is indirect evidence. You should think about your questions carefully and make a conscious decision about what type of evidence is most important to you. Thoughtful planning when developing the protocols will be required to gather the type of information you want as evidence.

Order and Content
Bogdan and Biklen (1998) suggest that protocol questions should be ordered carefully such that the participants are put at ease during the interview or focus group. The first part of the interview or focus group should be introductions. According to Bogdan and Biklin (1998), during this time the interviewers or moderators should take the time to introduce themselves and describe their role. In focus groups, this should include the note taker (Krueger, 1998). After introductions, the interviewers or moderators should explain the purpose of the study, the topics to be covered and, if appropriate, the ground rules that apply (Krueger, 1998). If you are required to obtain permission to do the study by your campus human subjects review board, you may be required to read specific information and possibly obtain a signature indicating that they are aware of certain aspects of the study. Bogdan and Biklen go on to suggest that confidentiality be addressed so that the participants know exactly what types of information will be shared and in what ways. If the subject is at all sensitive, this is extremely important. This may help put the interviewee or focus group members at ease, making it more likely that they will share detailed information. During this time, you should explain that you will be audiotaping the interview or focus group and ask them for permission. It is

important to explain that you are taping so that you will have an accurate record for analysis but that individual responses will still be kept confidential (Bogdan & Biklen, 1998).

LeCompte and Preissle (1993) refer to the ordering and wording of questions as "scripting" (p. 172). When ordering questions, they suggest taking several issues into consideration. One issue to consider is complexity. If the topic is highly complex, start with simple questions and work towards the more complex. If two or more topics are similar, place them together on the protocol. This will help with the flow of the interview. If two topics that are similar are discussed at very different times within the protocol, it may appear as if your thoughts are not organized. If appropriate, you may want to order the topics across a timeline. If you are asking questions regarding issues that took place in some specific order, it might be more appropriate to organize the protocol in that way. If the participant(s) seem to be interested in one topic more than others, it might be best to start with what they are interested in talking about. This may also put them at ease and help develop rapport with the interviewer. If there are risky or sensitive topics, it might be best to put those towards the middle or end of the interview or focus group. The participants may be more willing to answer those questions once they are at ease and rapport has been developed through the earlier conversations (LeCompte & Preissle, 1993).

Wording

While less structured interviews and focus groups may use topics instead of prewritten questions (Patton, 2002), it is still a good idea to practice how you intend to talk about an issue so that you ask open-ended questions and avoid leading participants to a particular answer. Practicing questions may also help in identifying common language. It is important to avoid the use of jargon whenever possible (Krueger, 1998).

Debriefing

The closing of an interview or focus group may seem abrupt to participants, so offering a debriefing is a good way to bring closure (Krueger, 1998). A debriefing may include thanking the participant(s) for attending, reminding them of the purpose of the study, reinforcing that their information will be kept confidential, and asking for permission to contact them for clarity as you analyze the information gathered. This simple exercise

may bring closure for those that desire to continue conversation about the issue.

Preparation: Where Will You Conduct Your Interview or Focus Groups?

An important tip for good interviews and focus groups is to choose your location wisely. A quiet location with few distractions is ideal (Patton, 2002). Avoid public places such as coffee shops or lounges and avoid places with ringing phones and interruptions from coworkers and friends. Not only are these things distracting but also the result may be an inaudible tape recording.

In addition to avoiding noise and other human distractions, be certain that the room is an appropriate size. Focus groups that are crammed into small spaces or interviews between two people that are in very large rooms can cause distraction as well. Keep this in mind when making room reservations (Krueger, 1998).

Preparation for Interviewing or Moderating

Walking into an interview or focus group unprepared is likely to result in an unproductive session. Krueger (1998) offers a number of suggestions to avoid this problem. Krueger suggests that the persons conducting the session prepare mentally for the conversation. When conducting any kind of interview, especially focus groups, you must be able to respond quickly to new ideas and ask appropriate follow-up questions. This is difficult to do if you are distracted by a poorly set up room or lacking equipment or documentation. Arriving early to check the room and developing a checklist of items you will need are both ways to avoid distraction during the session. Reviewing the purpose of the study and practicing the introduction and questions are also great ways to ensure that the session will go smoothly.

Conducting the Interview or Focus Group: Tips for Establishing Rapport

Establishing rapport has been mentioned several times thus far and is essential to a successful interview or focus group. If rapport is not established, students may not be comfortable providing you with all the information they hold on a subject. Once an interview or focus group has begun, there are a number of things the interviewer or moderator can do to ensure a successful session. Krueger (1998), Marshall and Rossman (1999), and Glesne (1999) all discuss the importance of certain interviewer or moderator behaviors. Establishing rapport includes speaking clearly, showing genuine interest,

54

controlling body language, remembering the role of the interviewer or moderator, staying on track, and seeking clarification.

Speak Clearly

Interviewers and moderators must speak clearly (Krueger, 1998). It is difficult for participants to respond when they do not understand the instructions or questions. This may make participants uncomfortable, and they may not ask clarifying questions.

Show Interest

Students need to know that you are listening to their responses (Glesne, 1999). You can show interest by maintaining eye contact, sitting up straight, and leaning in slightly.

Control Negative Body Language

It is entirely possible that you will be presented with information that makes you uncomfortable or even offended during an interview or focus group. It may be that you disagree with a view, students may provide the wrong answer to a knowledge-based question, or they may provide you with negative feedback about something you are responsible for creating. Regardless of why you are unhappy with a response, it is extremely important that you do not let the participant know how you feel about what they have said (Krueger, 1998). Body language and facial expressions are the first clues to participants that they may have said something to upset you. If they get that message they are unlikely to continue to be honest, and that will destroy your work. It is not easy to control body language or facial expressions, so practice it with someone who will provide you with honest feedback.

Remember Your Role

As educators, it is difficult to suppress the teacher inside. When you are acting as an interviewer or moderator, you must be willing to do so. Your role is to gather information about your subject, not to educate participants on the issues you are discussing. If you fall into this role you will likely negatively affect your ability to gather accurate data. If you start correcting students as they provide you with information, they may shut down. When they realize that the answers they are giving are "wrong" in some way, they may stop participating honestly. Remember that the purpose of your interview or focus group is to gather information about your outcome. If they are not comfortable answering questions honestly, you will not know if an outcome is met. There are ethical issues involved, of course. You need to decide prior to the interviews or focus groups how you will handle situations in which you feel the need to step in and provide additional information to students. One possibility is to wait and talk with the student(s) after the session is over. In this scenario, the student receives the correct information and the interview or focus group is not compromised. If other ethical dilemmas arise, we suggest you contact the office that is responsible for reviewing and approving research for suggestions on how to handle them.

Another damaging consequence of forgetting your role is that you are not able to gather the information you wanted because you got off track. Valuable time may be lost as you explore interesting but unrelated topics. For example, if you have a background dealing with student alcohol consumption and during an interview or focus group that issue arises and you pursue it when it is not why you are talking with the participant (s), you will likely lose the opportunity to talk with them about the outcomes you are measuring.

Stay on Track

Keeping participants on track during interview or focus groups can be much more difficult than you would imagine. Students may start to answer a question and then head off onto an unforeseen tangent. Brining them back, very gently, to the topic at hand is important. In focus groups it is even more difficult because other students may want to continue with the unrelated discussion. One strategy is to explain to the participant(s) that while the topic is very interesting, you need to try to stay on track so that you can get their input on all the issues (Krueger, 1998).

Seek Clarification

While staying on track is important, you may need to ask follow-up questions to clarify someone's response (Patton, 2002). At times you may not be sure if you should redirect a student back on topic or if you should pursue what may appear to be an off track comment. It is important not to assume you know what the student intends. In some cases you need to ask follow-up questions to clarify a student's definition of a commonly used term. For example, if a student is talking about a confrontation with a student on the hall and the participant says the student was disrespectful, you might ask the participant to define "disrespectful." You can do so by asking for clarification regarding specific behaviors that indicated disrespect. This information will help you frame the participant's response to the student on the hall and assist in determining if the student's confrontation skills are appropriate.

Common Concerns

When conducting interviews or focus groups, it is possible that you will encounter participants that challenge you. Krueger (1998) categorizes challenges in terms of personality types. He suggests that interviewers or moderators be aware of the "expert," "dominant talker," "extremely shy participant," "disruptive group member," and "rambler" (Krueger, 1998, pp. 58–64). When these personality types are encountered (most commonly in focus groups), there are effective ways to manage them.

One of the first agenda items on the protocol should be to set up ground rules (Krueger, 1998). This is not common in interviews but very common in focus groups. Setting ground rules at the beginning may help deter some negative behaviors. Asking that the participants speak one at a time, listen to others, refrain from using foul language, and respect that others have different opinions may stop some participants from engaging in difficult behavior before they start.

If they are the expert, dominant talker, or rambler, they usually share more often than others in the group. One way to handle this is to reaffirm your appreciation for their contribution, but then look to the group and state that you would like to hear from others (and sometimes you are forced to do this several times) (Krueger, 1998). This usually sends the message to these personality types that other people need to have a turn to respond. It is very important to be prepared for these situations. Because we were only able to briefly discuss this issue, you should consider reading Krueger's (1998) focus group book series prior to leading a group.

Note Taking

Why take notes if you are going to tape record an interview or focus group? This is a common question and one that we are happy to answer. One very important reason to take notes in addition to taping is that tapes fail and fail often, as we have learned from personal experience. Sometimes the tape is bad to begin with, so all you get is static. Sometimes the tape is demagnetized at some point after the recording is made. Sometimes sections of the tape are inaudible for no apparent reason (and sometimes for obvious reasons). And sometimes they are lost, stolen, or eaten by the dog. There are many reasons that you could lose the data you expect to have on a tape. Having notes as backup is extremely helpful.

Notes taken during interviews or focus groups should be very comprehensive (Patton, 2002). Do not let the fact that the tape is running lull you into a false sense of security. Take notes as if the tape is not there, and include information that the tape will miss. Notes not only include content about the conversation but also about body language, facial expressions, and apparent mood. This information may be important when you are analyzing your data from transcripts. In individual interviews, the interviewer takes notes. When conducting focus groups there should be a note taker so the moderator can focus on facilitating the conversation.

Analysis

Due to the large volume of text, data analysis of interview data or focus group data can easily be overwhelming. If you transcribe your tapes you may find that you have a tremendous amount of information. It is very difficult to know where to begin. Whether you are using your notes or transcripts, the first task is to organize your data. You can use three-ring binders, files, or whatever organizer makes sense to you.

The first questions to ask yourself are: What are you looking for? What are the outcomes being measured? If you interviewed looking for specific answers to questions (demonstrating specific knowledge), then you will use either a rubric or checklist to analyze what you found. More information regarding rubrics and checklists can be found in Chapter Five.

If you are searching for information regarding a topic but have no particular criteria, you will most likely want to do open coding to pull themes from the data (Strauss & Corbin, 1990). If that is the case you will need to assign a numbering system to your raw data. This will help you keep track of pieces of information that you pull out as you code. For more information on coding, see Chapter Eleven.

Cost-saving Tips

Interviews and focus groups may seem like an affordable way to do assessment, and compared to other tools and methods, they are inexpensive. There are, however, a few costs that can become fairly significant depending on the number of interviews or focus groups you conduct. When budgeting for interviews and focus groups you should consider the equipment needed for audiotaping. You may need to buy a recorder, but in many cases you can borrow one from someone on campus. You should also budget for tapes. Tapes are not costly, and you can save money by using both sides.

The biggest cost of interviews and focus groups are transcription costs. Depending on the length of the interviews and focus groups and the number of participants in the focus groups, the cost can be exorbitant. One way to save money is to transcribe the tapes yourself (Table 8–1). You should be cautioned that while this will save you significant money, it will cost you time. Transcribing the tapes yourself is a slow and very tedious process, but the benefit is that you will become very familiar with your data. If you do not have money for someone to transcribe and no time to do it yourself, you could use your notes for your data and the tape as back up. We would suggest listening to your tape and filling in your notes as much as possible before coding. Then when you use direct quotes, verify them with the tape. This will reduce the likelihood of inaccurate quotes or interpretations.

If you want to use incentives but do not have the funding, ask for donations from the bookstore or off campus vendors. You can use the donations for a drawing. Another way to pay for items for a drawing or to fund transcripts is to apply for small research grants through a professional organization or through a division in your university.

TABLE 8–1

Cost-saving Tips

- Transcribe tapes yourself or use your notes as your raw data, and then use the tapes as backup and quality check.
- Ask for donations from local vendors for incentives.
- Research possible grants for additional funding.

As mentioned previously, this information is not exhaustive of the literature on interviews and focus groups. The intention was to provide some basic information that can help you in determining the methods that will be useful in your assessment of student learning. For more information on interviews and focus groups, please refer to the References and Bibliography sections of this book.

CHAPTER 9

Observations and Documents

Observations

Observations are another example of an underused (and free) assessment technique. They can be used to measure an array of outcomes, but we will focus on student learning and development outcomes.

Example Outcomes

Following are examples of outcomes that can be measured with observations:

1) Resident advisors (RAs) will demonstrate effective and appropriate confrontation skills.

2) Students will demonstrate rock climbing safety skills.

3) Student Activities will create a sense of university community through their programs.

These outcomes are examples from Housing, Campus Recreation, and Student Activities. Some relate to student staff learning and development, and others relate to student learning and development through programming on campus. Observations can be used to determine if the outcomes have been meet and to assist in determining ways to improve the unit.

Description

What is an "observation?" If you were to review qualitative literature on observations you would find that there is a broad range of research designs associated with observing people, cultures, or phenomenon (Glesne, 1999). The term "participant observation" can refer to a complex research design involving an in-depth study of a culture or phenomenon that often includes living with, working with, and watching all aspects of the culture (LeCompte & Preissle, 1999). It can also simply refer to a method for gathering data when the observer

participates in the event being observed. LeCompte and Preissle (1999) discuss the varying levels of the observers' involvement when observing. In some situations, the observer will not only participate in the day-to-day life of the observed, the observer will ask the participants to review the day's notes for accuracy and to note any of the observers' misperceptions. In other cases, observers watch from the outside. They are neutral and uninvolved and have virtually no direct contact with the participants. Observations are often used in combination with other methods such as case studies, interviews, and focus groups.

For the purpose of most assessment activities, observations will usually be much more simplistic but still have many of the benefits of more involved observations. Patton (2002) discusses three strengths of observations. One is that "through direct observations the inquirer is better able to understand and capture the context within which people interact. Understanding context is essential to a holistic perspective" (2002, p. 262). The second is that observer "has less need to rely on prior conceptualizations of the setting" (2002, p. 262). And the third is that the observer "has the opportunity to see things that may routinely escape awareness among the people in the setting" (2002, p. 262).

Basic Implementation

Having noted the complex nature of observations and various ways to implement them, there are less complex ways to apply this methodology to assessment in the cocurricular. Observations can provide direct evidence of student learning and development as it is applied to real situations. It is important to remember, however, that while using observations for assessment may be at times more simplistic than in qualitative studies of entire cultures, there are still procedures to follow to ensure accurate recording of information and interpretation to increase the credibility of the work.

When observing behavior, Berg (2001) suggests that the observer record key words and phrases and make notes about the sequence of the events. As soon as the observation is over, the observer should write a detailed set of notes. This should be done almost immediately so that data are not compromised by poor memory. In some cases, observers may use highly structured checklists to ensure that certain elements of the situation are recorded (Marshall & Rossman, 1999). These techniques should be used, in some format, to assess student learning and development.

1) RAs will demonstrate effective and appropriate confrontation skills.

When you consider the example outcomes provided earlier, there are multiple ways to use observations as a technique for assessing learning and development. Consider the first outcome: RAs will demonstrate effective and appropriate confrontation skills.

In assessing this outcome, observations can be used to determine if RAs have learned and are able to apply effective and appropriate confrontation skills. One of the RA's responsibilities is to roam the halls (referred to as "rounds") and confront issues as they arise. The trainer or RA's supervisor could observe the RA in the job setting. This could be done in one of several ways. The supervisor could choose to be an outside observer and follow the RA to observe the RA's confrontation skills without getting involved. Another possible approach is to attend the rounds with the RA, assist with several confrontations, and then slowly let the RA handle them alone. This approach would likely serve as a continuation of the training that occurred earlier in the semester while also allowing the RA to demonstrate effective and appropriate confrontation skills.

2) Students will demonstrate rock climbing safety skills.

Observations may be used in a similar manner to measure the second outcome: Students will demonstrate rock climbing safety skills. A "teaching while observing" approach may be taken to measure student learning of rock climbing safety skills. For example, if the Campus Recreation Department teaches a two-hour seminar on rock climbing, students learning the safety skills associated with rock climbing is a likely outcome. One possible scenario would be for the instructor to provide information, demonstrate the skills, assist students as they practice, and then observe the students as they take turns demonstrating what they have learned. The person teaching the skills may demonstrate them for the students, assist them while they try to do it themselves, and then observe the students as they take turns climbing.

3) Student Activities will promote a sense of university community through their programs.

The third outcome will require more complicated observation techniques: Student Activities will promote a sense of university community through their programs. To measure this outcome, observations may be made during Student Activities-sponsored programs, and the observer may take a participant role in the functions or act as a neutral third party observer. The observer may attend all the activities or a selection of activities and take detailed notes on all aspects of the events including details of the space used, individuals that attend, individuals that sponsor the program, and the interactions of all involved. A study designed to measure this outcome may include other measures such as interviews, focus groups, and tracking of attendance or other statistical information. The study would likely take at least one semester, if not longer, and may provide valuable information about how Student Activities impacts the sense of university community through programming. Depending on the criteria used to determine promoting a sense of community, the staff would review the data and make interpretations. They could then use the information to make improvements that would assist in promoting a sense of community.

Analysis

When measuring an outcome, there must be criteria to define the learning or development. The staff may define the criteria; there may be a more formal criteria based on literature, or in some cases the study itself defines the criteria to determine if an outcome was met. Depending on the kind of data collected during observations, analysis may involve a rubric or criteria checklist as described in Chapter Five or open coding and content analysis as described in Chapter Eleven.

In the RA and rock-climbing examples described previously, there are likely checklists or rubrics that would assist in determining if the RAs are "effectively and appropriately" confronting students and if the rock-climbing students are accurately applying the "safety skills" taught during the seminar. The observer may either take notes, then apply the criteria or rubric after the observation, or the observer may have the checklist or rubric at the time of the observation and determine if the criteria is met as the observations are occurring.

The Student Activities example may require a different approach. While observers can use criteria chosen by observers either from literature, student input, or a self-defined set of standards based on professional experience, they also may choose to rely on the observations to provide a definition of promoting a sense of university community through coding the data collected. If observers choose to use predetermined criteria, they can use it as the basis for a content analysis. If observers choose to use open coding, they will take the notes from all the observed activities and look for themes regarding the promotion of a sense of university community. Once the themes are identified, observers can either use the themes to discuss how Student Activities promotes a sense of university community or they can take coding one step further and use the themes as the criteria to perform content analysis to talk more specifically about how often the themes are occurring.

Document Analysis

Document Analysis is another underused method for assessing student learning and development, but it is an effective way to gather evidence. It is not difficult to do; can be used to measure several types of outcomes; and you may find that you learn a significant amount about your staff, organization, or students through the documentation of meetings and other events. Document analysis involves the gathering of documents such as minutes from organizational or staff meetings, reports, photographs, old letters, student files, or organizational files (Patton, 2002). When conducting document analysis, each document is carefully studied as if it were a piece of data you collected. It may be a tool you use as part of a case study or it may be a tool used to measure a specific outcome. One major benefit is that it is unobtrusive because it does not involve asking other people for time and energy and can often be implemented as time permits.

Example Outcomes

A new student organization was created to work closely with the Campus Women's Center to develop programs to meet the needs of the women students on campus. The student members were trained on women's issues and were provided research findings of a needs assessment on campus. They have been active for two semesters.

The Women's Center Staff has the following outcomes for the members:

- Student members will demonstrate leadership in the area of women's issues.

- Student members will demonstrate independence in determining appropriate programming.

- Student members will demonstrate the ability to implement successful programs.

One way the staff can determine if these outcomes have been met is to do a document analysis of the organizational minutes and files. In this case, the staff would gather copies of all the minutes from executive meetings and group meetings and all other organizational files. Keeping in mind the questions they are trying to answer, the staff would read through each page of the documents gathered and make detailed notes regarding what was in each set of minutes or files. In the meeting minutes and organizational files, you may find information regarding types of programs that are offered, who suggested them, who was responsible for what aspects, what went well and what did not, reports from members that attended other organizational meetings as a liaison, and more. This information can be analyzed to assist in determining if (1) the outcomes were met and (2) if they were not met, how the staff can refocus their efforts to improve in those areas.

For example, during the analysis, the staff found that while all the programs presented were "successful" based on their criteria, each of the programs were suggested by the staff instead of the students. In further analysis, the staff found that student members did suggest programs, but those programs were not implemented. In this case, the staff felt that the outcome of "demonstrating independence" was not met because the students relied on them to determine the best programming options. The staff may take that information and decide to change how they provide the students with programming ideas.

The minutes may also demonstrate that the organization has not been sending a representative to major campus-wide meetings or events in which they would have been able to represent the perspective of the organization. This may indicate, depending on the criteria, that the members are not fully demonstrating "leadership in the area of women's issues."

Another example for document analysis is the use of student files to determine growth. The Office of Student Conduct may have an outcome that states: Students that visit the Office of Student Conduct will demonstrate better decision-making skills.

A common measure of success for judicial programs is a low recidivism rate for students violating the Code. The recidivism rate, while it may indicate a problem for the campus if it is very high, will not advise the staff if a particular student is making better decisions. One way to find out if the outcome was being met would be to do a document analysis of the student's judicial file. The student file would likely contain the following documents: signed paperwork indicating if they completed all their sanctions and did so on time; a writing assignment that could be reviewed for content regarding thoughts on the decision that brought them to the office as well as subsequent decisions; information regarding academic standing before and after the incident; and staff notes regarding other conversations with the student, parents, and other involved people. Using the criteria for "better decision-making," the staff may be able to determine if the student is making better decisions. Using the initial meeting notes as the "pretest," the staff could make a determination if learning and development has occurred. Some of the information would be self-reported learning and development, such as the information gathered through the writing sample, while other information would provide direct evidence. For example, in many judicial cases, a major aspect of poor decision-making includes some

level of irresponsibility. Depending on the student, direct evidence of learning and development may be gathered from the file, such as evidence that the student completed all required sanctions on time and correctly and attended all required meetings with the staff.

Analysis

Analyzing data collected through document analysis may involve open coding, content analysis, or checklists using criteria (Marshall & Rossman, 1999; Patton, 2002). As stated in Chapters Five and Eleven, the decision regarding how to analyze the documents you are reviewing will be based on how criteria are applied. If there is a predetermined list of criteria, content analysis or checklists would be the best approach. If there is not a predetermined list and, based on the outcome being measured, themes developed through the data are most helpful, then open coding should be used. It is possible that content analysis or checklists may be applied later in the process. Regardless of which approach you take, it is best to determine how you will analyze the data in advance. See Chapters Five and Eleven for more information on analyzing data.

Observations and document analysis are great tools for gathering rich detailed information. If, based on the outcome being measured, one or both are used to assess learning and development, the assessor is likely to have an abundance of wonderful information to use for decision-making. If prior to implementing either technique you are interested in learning more about them, please review the list of resources for more detailed information.

CHAPTER 10

Case Studies

What is a Case Study?

There are two basic definitions of case studies as they may be applied to assessment of student learning and development. The first definition is much more broad and involves a fairly complicated methodology. The second definition involves using a written situation as a teaching technique as well as an assessment technique.

Case Studies as a Method

To choose a case study format is to commit to a very detailed inquiry into a person, place, organization, time of life, process, specific incident, or program. Marshall and Rossman (1999, p. 159) state "Case studies take the reader into the setting with a vividness and detail not typically present in more analytic reporting formats." Case studies involve multiple methods of data gathering, most of which are discussed in some detail in this book. Case studies include interviews; observations; document analysis; and possibly focus groups, relevant statistics, and other contextual information. Patton (2002) refers to a case study as a process that ultimately produces a product. Essentially, the "case study" is also the product; it is the analysis and synthesis of all the data collected from multiple methods during the study.

Case Studies as a Teaching Technique

Another definition of case study involves a teaching technique that allows students to explore a realistic situation by analyzing and interpreting the information they are given. The students then apply what they have learned in a class or cocurricular activity to appropriately resolve or respond to the situation (e.g., the case study) (Huba & Freed, 2000). In many situations, the students have an opportunity to write a response or discuss the case and all the possible resolutions or responses as a group. This provides the students with an opportunity to teach each other as well as informally evaluate each others' ability to apply what was learned.

Implementation

Case Studies as a Method

When using the case study as a method of studying something or someone, there are a number of ways to structure the research. Usually a single "case" is chosen as the topic of study such as one person or one organization, although it is not always that simple. Patton (2002) suggests that case studies can be "nested" (p. 447). He reminds us that while doing a case study of an organization, we can also do a case study of one or more individuals within the organization or of a particular activity that is part of the organization.

If you are not nesting your case, however, you will still gather data about the smallest unit. If you are doing a case study about an umbrella organization, you need to gather data about all the organizations that fall under the umbrella, even if you do not do a more formalized case study of one or more of the smaller organizations.

Gathering data for most cast studies will include interviews, document analysis, observations, and other methods. The use of multiple methods allows the assessor to view the subject under study from every aspect and compare and contrast the information gathered during analysis.

Case Studies as a Teaching Technique

If you are using a case study as a teaching technique, the case study materials need to be carefully compiled in a manner such that when the students respond to the situation presented to them (which may include narratives, relevant documents, and other appropriate artifacts), you are able to see the following in their work:

"understanding the situation being faced; analyzing the specific problem to be tackled; creating, analyzing, and refining a solution; and further evaluating, improving, and implementing" (Engineering Communication Centre, 2002, p. 1).

In addition to carefully composing the case study, you will want to be sure to make teaching and evaluation notes so that you can leverage the use of this tool both for delivering the outcome and for assessing the extent of the student's learning. In other words, when presenting the case study to the students, you want to make sure that it contains all that you wish for the students to learn. The list of what you want them to learn may be in the form of a criteria checklist or rubric (see Chapter Five). Furthermore, when you begin to evaluate whether the students have learned what you wanted them to learn, or whether they evaluate each other, they can use the initial criteria checklist, as well as any other points that you may have discovered they are learning.

Why Choose a Case Study?

Case Studies as a Method
Brief as it is, the abovementioned information may have readers wondering why they should engage in a case study as a methodology, as it sounds like an enormous undertaking. It is true that case studies are comprehensive and involve a lot of planning and devotion of time to fully implement the process. In addition, analyzing the data will be more complicated because there are multiple methods. It is important to remember, however, that depending on the questions being asked, a case study may provide the most comprehensive information for decision-making regarding student learning and development. The rich data collected, the pervasiveness of the methods used, and the intense planning involved will also lend credibility to the work.

Case Studies as a Teaching Technique
Choosing to use a case study as a teaching technique requires time to write it well and plan for its use in both teaching and assessment. However, it is an efficient way in which to both teach and assess. For example, case studies can be written to evaluate students' ability to identify and resolve situations involving dilemmas with academic integrity, civic responsibility, discrimination, engagement, and leadership. These case studies can be administered and evaluated in a span of two hours. This enables students to engage in debate, allowing for

further education on the subject as well as providing you a rich context for evaluation (Huba & Freed, 2000).

Example Outcomes
There are a number of situations for which we might use a case study to determine if we met an outcome. It may also be used when we determine that we are not meeting an outcome, and we still need to know more about what is happening.

In Chapter Nine we talked about the following situation:

A new student organization was created to work closely with the Campus Women's Center to develop programs to meet the needs of the women students on campus. The student members were trained on women's issues and were provided research findings of a needs assessment on campus. They have been active for two semesters.

The Women's Center Staff has the following outcomes for the members:

- Student members will demonstrate leadership in the area of women's issues.

- Student members will demonstrate independence in determining appropriate programming.

- Student members will demonstrate the ability to implement successful programs.

The staff started measuring these outcomes by engaging in document analysis of minutes from meetings and other important organizational paperwork. In Chapter Nine, we illustrated that they found some evidence of meeting two outcomes. If the staff had found no evidence of leadership, independence, or implementation of successful programming, they may have decided to take a step back and study the entire organization. Instead of measuring a specific outcome(s), they may decide to review all aspects of the organization to find out how they are operating and why the outcomes measured thus far have not been met. In this situation, a case study of the organization will include a document analysis; but instead of looking only for the outcomes, the documents would be studied using open coding as described in Chapter Eleven in order to identify themes. In addition to the more comprehensive document analysis, other data would be gathered. For example, the student executive board and members, Women's Center staff, and the advisor of the organization might be interviewed; and the staff member conducting the case study may choose to observe meetings and programs and review statistical information regarding membership, programming, and other data.

The analysis of this information would provide details regarding the organization and assist the staff in determining if the outcomes for the group are still relevant. If the outcomes are determined to be relevant, the staff may also learn how they should improve so that the students learn and develop as they have stated in the outcomes. The staff may also find that due to what they learn about the organization, they need to make changes to the mission and objectives of the organization and that additional learning and developmental outcomes need to be created.

Example: Implementing a Nested Case Study

A Residence Life program developed objectives and learning and development outcomes associated with the resident director (RD) level graduate students that are responsible for managing the residence halls on campus. While attempting to measure the outcomes, they realized that there was a significant amount of premature turnover in the staff. Residence Life was committed to hiring graduate students because they believed in providing support to Student Affairs graduate students and thought the training opportunity was invaluable. Unsure as to why the turnover was occurring, the office decided to invest in a case study analysis of the life of a new RD.

In Residence Life, RDs are responsible for running a hall of undergraduate students while balancing a full graduate level academic course load. RDs have a staff of undergraduate Resident Assistants (RAs) to assist them. RAs are assigned a floor of students for which they are responsible for basic counseling, discipline, mail distribution, programming, and facilities.

RDs report to full-time assistant directors. The assistant directors are responsible for a collection of residence halls and supervise five to seven RDs, all facilities staff, and other support staff. Due to the nature of the RDs' work, case studies of at least one RA and one assistant director would be appropriate to fully understand the relationships. In addition, the assessor would need to gather data regarding the university, Residence Life program, and the graduate program. The assessor would observe meetings, programs, and training as well as interview a variety of the people the RD works with or comes in contact with as part of their graduate experience. Document analysis of files, forms, reports, evaluations, and other appropriate paperwork would also be

important in understanding the RD experience. This information could then be used to improve the RD experience and ultimately the long-term impact on the RD's learning and development.

Analysis

Case Studies as a Method

As mentioned earlier, the "case study" is not only a process but also a product. To form case study data into a case study product, careful analysis is required. Patton (2002) suggests that the assessor develop a case report. A case report is a comprehensive collection of the data after it has been reviewed and condensed. Duplicate and irrelevant information is be stripped from the raw data so that an organized report exists. If the study is nested, review each of the smaller case studies first using the analysis methods described in Chapters Five and Eleven. In most cases open coding is used to develop themes in the data so that a narrative can be written. After the analysis, the last stage is developing a meaningful narrative that describes the findings of the case study. The narrative tells a story about the subject and provides information that is useful for improvement. It can be chronological or organized by issues or themes. Regardless of how it is organized, the material indicates that the study was holistic (Patton, 2002; Stake, 1995).

Case Studies as a Teaching Technique

When using a case study as a teaching technique, the data gathered will be in the form of the student's response to the scenario. This data can then be analyzed using a rubric or criteria checklist (see Chapter Five). You can present individual data analysis in a summary form of what you observed or what the peers observed as the key learning principles and the areas in which the student needs to improve. The individual data can be summarized in a holistic manner as well provide you with an overview of what you need to improve in your program. This type of analysis allows for individual improvement in student performance as well as improvement in the overall program.

Cost-saving Tips

Case Studies as a Method

Case studies are comprehensive, so they will take a lot of time to complete and will likely be expensive. Unfortunately, to conduct a comprehensive case study, time is required. Money may be saved using some of the techniques mentioned in Chapter Eleven. Transcribing tapes yourself or using the notes with the tapes as backup for verification will save money, as paying for transcripts is very costly.

Case Studies as a Teaching Technique

Case studies used as a teaching technique are very cost effective. The largest resource investment involves the time spent writing them well. Books on case studies such as Merriam's (1997) *Qualitative Research and Case Study Applications in Education: Revised and Expanded from Case Study Research in Education* can be used, and case studies from several disciplines may be borrowed and adapted to your specific needs. In addition, it may be helpful to consult Barbazette's (2003) book entitled *Instant Case Studies for Successful Trainers: Adapt, Use, and Create Your Own Case Studies* to assist you in writing your own case studies.

Summary

In summary, case studies are a comprehensive way to gather detailed data about all aspects of a position or organization. The process will provide a greater understanding of all factors that have an effect on the subject and the subject itself, and therefore will provide some clarity on how to proceed with the recommended improvements. Planning is important and a dedicated, long-term approach is necessary. While case studies do not occur overnight, the results will likely provide what you need to make quality decisions regarding the subject of study. The following resources may be useful in learning more about case studies, and you are encouraged to review them prior to conducting a case study project.

CHAPTER 11

Analyzing Qualitative Data

For the purpose of this chapter and the tools discussed in the book, we have chosen to discuss Patton's (2002), Berg's (2001), and other researchers' views on (and relationships between) content analysis and coding and how they can be applied to assessment of student learning and development. If you would like more detailed information regarding their views or the views of others, you will find a list of references and additional resources at the end of the book. The term "coding" refers to organizing and making sense of textual information resulting from a study by determining themes in the data (Bogdan & Biklen, 1998). This is a rather simplified version of Strauss and Corbin's (1990) definitions of open coding, axial coding, and selective coding, which are often used in combination. According to Strauss and Corbin (1990) these three concepts involve "breaking down, examining, comparing, conceptualizing and categorizing data" (p. 61); then putting data "back together in new ways . . . by making connections between categories" (p. 96); and, finally, "selecting the core category, systematically relating it to other categories, validating those relationships, and filling in categories that need further refinement and development" (p. 116).

Traditionally, the term "content analysis" is used to describe a more quantitative process that involves determining how often themes and patterns occur and then representing the findings numerically (Babbie, 1990). In his work on qualitative methodology, Berg (2001) discusses disagreements regarding the terms and confirms that they are often labeled as distinctly qualitative or quantitative. Berg suggests that the two concepts of coding and content analysis are related and states, "The categories researchers use in a content analysis can be determined inductively, deductively, or by some combination of both" (Berg, 2001, p. 245). We will start this discussion with the development of themes through

coding and then the application of content analysis. This approach is based on Patton's (2002) and Berg's (2001) suggestion that coding may be used to develop the themes and patterns that may later be used in content analysis. There may be times when themes are identified in some other fashion, but using coding of qualitative data to determine the categories for content analysis is a commonly used and supported strategy (Patton, 2002; Berg, 2001).

Open Coding: A Quick Guide

Open coding is a term used to describe the determination of themes from within the data (Patton, 2002). It is a common method of analyzing qualitative data, most specifically interview, observations, and focus group data. In describing qualitative data analysis, Bogdan and Biklen (1998) state, "The process of data analysis is like a funnel: Things are open at the beginning (or top) and more directed and specific at the bottom. The qualitative researcher plans to use part of the study to learn what the important questions are. He or she does not assume that enough is known to recognize important concerns before undertaking the research" (p. 7).

In open coding, you are trying to identify themes and sub-themes within the data. This can be an overwhelming task at first. However, it is quite rewarding as you watch themes develop. There are many styles of coding so we have devised a set of step-by-step instructions to get you started.

Coding: Step One—After Data Collection
Reframe: re-familiarize yourself with the purpose of the study (Marshall & Rossman, 1999). As described in Chapter Eleven, participants sometimes go off on tangents. To avoid following that same tangent as you try to make sense of your data, ask yourself what are you

trying to find out. In other words, review your outcome statements. What is it that you expected students to learn or to know? This may sound unnecessary, but it is very easy to get distracted by data that is unrelated to the study.

Coding: Step Two
If you are coding interviews or focus groups, listen to the tapes to verify transcripts and read the data once without trying to identify themes (Patton, 2002). If you are coding written data, such as observation notes or documents, reread the materials. If you have conducted a large number of interviews or focus groups, or if some time has passed since you finished data collection, this will re-familiarize you with the entire set of data.

Coding: Step Three
Reread your data and take preliminary notes regarding patterns on a separate sheet of paper or in the margins. This is the beginning stage of organizing themes. You might find it useful to number your data so that if you start to transfer quotes or pieces of information onto a separate sheet of paper, you will have a way to track where you originally found that piece of data. You will then use the notes to develop a primitive outline or system of classifications into which data are sorted initially. Marshall and Rossman (1999) describe this as the broad regularities you see that will inform the first categories. "The researcher does not search for the exhaustive and mutually exclusive categories of the statistician but, instead, identifies the salient, grounded categories of meaning held by participants in the setting" (Marshall & Rossman, 1999, p. 154).

Krueger (1994) suggests that researchers consider other factors when coding and analyzing data. When reviewing data, you should not only consider the words on the document or used by the participants, but also the meaning of the words. A variety of words will have the same meaning, therefore falling into the same category. When dealing with interviews or focus groups, you should consider the comment or question that triggered a particular response and the tone used by the participant. Note takers should make notes of any changes in tones that are striking. The tape can then be reviewed to determine if the meaning of the comment is in question based on tone.

When reviewing data, take note of changes in opinions or positions. This may occur within one focus group or interview, or you may notice changes in positions over time though meeting minutes. Pay special attention to

this for two reasons. One reason is that you do not want to inadvertently represent the same person's varying opinions as two opposing opinions. The second reason is that the change itself may be an important piece of information that informs what you know about the person, group, or organization.

Take note of the "frequency or extensiveness" (p. 150) and passion of certain responses. Again this may inform your interpretation of the comment. With document analysis you will likely not have this information if the documents are summaries, but you will have access if good notes were taken during observations and you have tapes of your interviews or focus groups.

Responses that are more specific may be more important than vague comments. But at the same time, you want to be careful not to miss the big picture because you are so closely analyzing each individual comment.

Coding: Step Four
Continue rereading the text and developing more detailed sub-themes or patterns within themes while highlighting the quotes that are relevant. Again, it is helpful to track the line numbers if you are using a separate sheet of paper to list themes and sub-themes. It is extremely frustrating to pull out a quote and then decide that you need more of the context but cannot find it in the transcript or notes! You can waste hours of time if you are not properly organized.

Coding: Step Five
Remove text related to the themes and reassemble by themes and sub-themes on a separate sheet of paper (Marshall & Rossman, 1999). If you have kept track of themes by using the line numbers, simply go back to the original documents and use the numbers to locate the data. This exercise will give you a more complete picture of the themes, sub-themes, and corresponding data that support them.

Ways to Ensure Quality When Identifying Themes
While we have repeatedly said that we are not attempting to provide the most rigorous of methodologies, that does not mean that when a tool is implemented we should not do our best to ensure high-quality work. Qualitative research has many critics in part because the critics do not understand the methodology, but also in part because there are those that conduct interviews and focus groups and simply pull out the information that they "feel" is most important. As you now know

after reading this chapter, if done properly, there is a lot more to analyzing qualitative research.

Once you have completed your identification of themes and coding of the data, there are two other analysis methods you can employ to help ensure that you kept an open mind and did not allow your biases to impede your identification of themes. One method is to look for what Marshall and Rossman (1999) refer to as "emergent understandings" (p. 157). As new patterns emerge during the identification of themes and coding, the researcher re-reviews earlier data to ensure that nothing was missed. This is not a difficult thing to do, and it allows you to be sure that you did not skim over any important information, especially when dealing with large volumes of data.

In situations involving sensitive or personal issues that may stay on your mind long after you leave work for the day, you might want to consider keeping personal memos. Many of us have revelations about our work at odd times such as 3:00 A.M. when we cannot sleep, while in the shower, and when we are walking the dogs. Personal memos are designed to keep track of those random thoughts about the data and allow us to separate our personal reactions from the analysis when appropriate (Marshall & Rossman, 1999).

The last quality control method described by both LeCompt and Preissle (1993) and Marshall and Rossman (1999) is to conduct negative case analysis. This strategy involves reviewing the data for information that conflicts with what you have identified as themes. You then take the time to see if you have missed a theme or if the information constitutes an anomaly. If it is an anomaly, reflect on why it exists and if it is important to the study.

Once you have a clearly developed set of themes and possibly sub-themes, you are able to describe what you have found with confidence. In open coding, it is not necessary to count exactly about how often a theme emerged in the data. Once you identify a theme in the data, you can discuss how it relates to the outcome(s) you are measuring. In some cases, once you have developed your themes and patterns (sub-themes), you may find content analysis useful.

Content Analysis

In content analysis, the textual data is reviewed and the information is categorized and counted (Patton, 2002). Content analysis may be an extension of themes developed during open-coding, or it may be based on a predetermined set of criteria either developed by the staff or through literature. Berg (2001) lists seven elements of text that might be counted as part of a content analysis: words, themes, characters, paragraphs, items, concepts, and semantics. When choosing content units, you may choose one unit, such as themes, or you may choose more than one unit, such as themes and characters. This process will look slightly different based on the topic and type of study. Content analysis may be especially useful in observations and document analysis or if those who will read the data will be more impacted by numerical information. Once the data is categorized and counted, it can be presented in a number of forms including graphs and charts. Depending on who will be reading your data, this may be an important consideration. For more detailed information regarding content analysis, see Berg's (2001) text on qualitative methods.

CHAPTER 12

Survey Research

What is a Survey?

A survey is a social scientific research method that typically involves selecting a random sample of people to answer some questions, selecting or designing a standardized questionnaire to get information about the research question(s), systematically administering the questionnaire, coding the responses in a standardized form, analyzing the results to provide descriptions about the people in the sample and find relationships between different responses, and generalizing the results to the population from which the sample was drawn (Babbie, 1990). Once you select the method of survey research, you then must select the type of survey.

Basic formats for surveys include self-administered mail surveys, telephone interviews, face-to-face interviews, focus groups, self-administered web surveys, and self-administered email surveys. The survey format largely determines much of the research design (e.g., sampling, questionnaire design, administration, data analysis, decisions-made) (Whelchel, 2002). Surveys and survey research is familiar territory; however, when using surveys for assessment, there are some key matters to which we must pay attention.

Surveys may be used with poor research design. In doing so, it invites criticism and misinterpretation of data and thus poor decision-making. If you want to maintain academic rigor in your assessment practice, pay attention to sound survey methodology, particularly to that of demonstrating good practices in sample size (Kuh, personal communication, 2003).

First, Articulate the Outcomes

When assessment is first mentioned, curricular and cocurricular professionals alike immediately consider using surveys. Often, as was illustrated briefly in Chapter Four, surveys are selected as an assessment method prior to articulating any program, student learning, or development outcomes. Since assessment's primary purpose is to gather information about whether your program is meeting specific intended end results so that you know what to improve, it is imperative that you first articulate your program's outcomes prior to administrating or designing any survey.

After having articulated your outcomes, there is a wealth of survey literature and accompanying surveys to assist you in measuring the extent to which you have achieved many of those outcomes. When choosing which survey to use or deciding to design one of your own, it is extremely helpful to base your survey choice decision upon that information which you are seeking.

Things to Consider When Making a Choice

We will provide you with information on where to find standardized surveys and with resources to consult when designing your own survey. But first, the following is a list of things to consider when choosing a survey or designing your own survey:

- Articulate the outcomes, which you are trying to measure. We know you have heard this many times, but we simply cannot stress this enough. We have witnessed commitment to assessment unravel as institutions invest in the administration and analyzing of surveys, only to discover that the surveys they chose shed no light on what they were trying to find out about their programs. Furthermore, the surveys they chose gave them very little information for knowing what to improve.

- In addition to the questions in Chapter Four, also consider the questions offered at this site: http://trochim.human.cornell.edu/kb/survsel.htm. These questions, addressing population, sampling, question construction, bias avoidance, and administration and content issues, are designed to assist you in choosing the most appropriate survey methodology for any study.

- Examine the psychometric properties of the survey instruments themselves. As we mentioned, there are a number of surveys to consider when assessing particular student learning and development outcomes. Psychometric properties tell you about the validity, reliability, stability, and other important measurability effects of particular instruments. An example of an informative psychometric properties page can be found on the National Survey of Student Engagement (NSSE) at http://www.indiana.edu/~nsse/html/faqpsych.shtml.

- Consider whether or not you will want to compare your survey results with those from other institutions, your peer institutions, or even among departments within your college or university. If you do want to obtain comparative data, then you will want to make sure you are using an instrument that offers comparative information, such as the benchmarking surveys of NSSE or Educational Benchmarking Incorporated. Another option is to work with institutions or departments for which you desire to compare information, in order to share in the exchange of similar instrument data.

- Sometimes scoring and interpreting standardized tests that assess certain student learning and development attributes is not easy. Be sure to find out as much as you are able about the instrument and also find out if the provider of the instrument can analyze that data for you or offer some assistance with interpretation. For example, some may not be able to easily interpret the *Defining Issues Test* in order to assess the extent their program is contributing to students' development of moral reasoning. Since we are not focusing on appropriate and accurate quantitative data analysis in this book, please do consult the many resources on this topic if you have any questions. A good start to finding out what is what

is Trochim's *Research Methods Knowledge Base* found at http://trochim.human.cornell.edu/kb/

- Constructing a survey is not as easy as it sounds. We mentioned this already in Chapter Four, and we mention it again because we do not want you to underestimate this aspect. Being able to report sound psychometric properties for one survey often takes years for the design, refinement, and testing of each questionnaire. If your constituents want and desire for you to assess student learning and development with "proven" survey methods, than you may prefer not to create your own survey. However, if you just want to find out if students will self-report that they have learned that which you wanted your workshop to accomplish, than sometimes simply stating the learning outcomes and asking students to rank the degree to which they learned a particular outcome will suffice. An example of this is in Appendix D. It all goes back to point number one—what is it that you are trying to learn about your program from the survey?

- Many national surveys are available for your use, and many of them have sound psychometric properties that will provide you with the ability to compare your results with other institutions. However, not all of these surveys evaluate student learning and development. Keep this in mind as you make decisions about your overall assessment plan and your evaluative instruments. Sometimes it is extremely helpful to gather baseline data, such as that gathered by the Cooperative Institutional Research Program's Freshman Survey (http://www.gseis.ucla.edu/heri/cirp.html) so that later learning and development instruments can be interpreted in a meaningful manner.

- If you are unsure of what a survey will measure or unsure of whether it will measure a student learning attribute in the way in which your program has defined it (e.g., critical thinking means different things to different people and is implemented in different ways), consult with your university or college faculty who have expertise in the test and measurement area. While faculty members are always busy, we are confident that most would rather share their expertise with you than see you invest and implement a survey that you will find dissatisfactory.

- Coordinate the administration and dissemination of surveys. Many students become "over-surveyed" because administrators are not paying attention to what surveys are being conducted on campus. Oftentimes, the formation of an assessment task force or the coordination of surveys through an institutional review board can save students from being "over-assessed" (Kuh, personal communication, 2003). However, communication among those planning to administer even a one-minute comment card is helpful in order to keep students from feeling "bombarded" with questions.

- Similar to the previous point, another challenge is to make sure that you do not administer the same survey year after year if it is not necessary to do so. "With a good sample and instrument, results shouldn't change much from one year to the next" (Kuh, personal communication, 2003). In addition, it may take time for the decisions to have an impact on the survey results. For example, if you learn from one year's survey that you need to improve a particular service in order to improve student learning, it may take an entire year to improve that service. Thus, administering the same survey in the next year may not be practical or appropriate.

Standardized Surveys

There are several high-quality standardized surveys from which to choose when assessing student-learning outcomes. The NSSE Survey has questions that could assist you with assessing any one of the following outcomes in addition to student engagement:

- Students will articulate a personal code of values and ethics.

- Students demonstrated a contribution to the welfare of their community.

- Students can identify when they work effectively with others.

- Students can illustrate similarities and differences in themselves and people of other racial and ethnic backgrounds.

The Your First College Year survey (University of California, Los Angeles Higher Education Research Institute, 2003) contains questions that will assist you with measuring outcomes such as:

- Students can discern the problems facing their communities.

- Students can articulate national and global issues.

- Students will identify their ability to work as part of a team.

Objectives Measures of Domains

There are also several high-quality objectives measures of domains. For example, if you are assessing outcomes related to critical thinking, and, depending on how you are defining critical thinking, you may want to use either the Watson-Glaser Critical Thinking Appraisal Survey (The Psychological Corporation, 2003), the California Critical Thinking Skills Test (2003), the California Critical Thinking Disposition Inventory (2003), or the Cornell Critical Thinking Test (2003). Again, if you articulate your outcomes prior to administering a survey, you not only know which survey will help you assess those outcomes better but you will also have a head start on the meaningful interpretation of that survey.

A list of standardized surveys and objectives measures of domains for use in assessing student learning and development can be found at the following websites:

- Assessment for Student Development Clearinghouse—http://www.acpa.nche.edu/comms/comm09/dragon/dragon-index.html

- Eric Clearinghouse for Assessment and Evaluation—http://ericae.net/ and http://ericae.net/nintbod.htm

- Western Psychological Association—http://www.westernpsych.org/

- North Carolina State University Internet Resources for Higher Education Outcomes Assessment (2003)—http://www2.acs.ncsu.edu/UPA/assmt/resource.htm

For assistance in comparing national standardized surveys, consult the article titled "Measuring Quality: Choosing Among Surveys and Other Assessments of College Quality" at http://www.airweb.org/images/measurequality.pdf.

Non-standardized Surveys

There are several books that discuss the "how-tos" of designing and administrating your own survey. Thus, we will not even attempt to cover that topic in this book. We will only provide an example. What is most important to remember here is what we have already discussed—that designing your own survey is not as easy as it sounds and, thus, appropriate time and attention need to be afforded to such an effort. Resources available to you to design and administer your own survey include the following:

- Babbie, E. (2002). *The basics of social research* (2nd ed.). Belmont, CA: Wadsworth Publishing.

- Dillman, D. A. (2000). *Mail and Internet surveys* (2nd ed.). NY: Wiley.

- Fink, A., & Kosecoff, J. (1998). *How to conduct surveys.* Thousand Oaks, CA: Sage Publications.

- Fowler, F. J. (1993). *Survey research methods.* Thousand Oaks, CA: Sage Publications.

- Fowler, F. J. (1995). *Improving survey questions.* Thousand Oaks, CA: Sage Publications.

- Sudman, S., & Bradburn, N. (1982). *A practical guide to questionnaire design.* San Francisco: Jossey-Bass.

- Tourangeau, R., & Smith, T. W. (1996). Asking sensitive questions: The impact of data collection mode, question format, and question context. *Public Opinion Quarterly, 60,* 275–304.

Non-standardized Surveys on Difficult Topics Like Diversity

Surveys and questionnaires provide valuable information from target groups concerning their characteristics, behaviors, beliefs, values, attitudes, and perceptions. They can be easily administered in person, by mail, or online. Surveys can address a range of topics, from those that seek to elicit responses to a limited range of topics to those that are more generic or cover a broad range.

Surveys are often more effective when respondents have some sense of the topic's meaning (unless the survey intent is otherwise). Yet, some topics are not always associated with traditional goals and objectives, or the subject matter for which there exists a prior agreement. Topics may be neutral in some situational contexts or

heightened in others. Moreover, the context may be campus-based or influenced by higher education trends. One concept that seems to produce a wide range of responses is the topic of diversity.

On many campuses diversity-related activities and programs are sponsored by cocurricular and curricular programs. Yet, such efforts are not always grounded in standards or criteria that increase the potential for success and the opportunity for effective assessment. The checklist in Appendix C incorporates criteria that can be associated with program effectiveness; moreover, it is based on the objective ratings of respondents.

A Mountain of Data

We realize that you may very well be reading this chapter because you have a mountain of data from some institutional survey that may have been analyzed but never used to inform decisions for continuous improvement. If this is the case, we want to provide you with a few tips for how to use that data in retrospect.

Identify positive aspects reported by the data. Describe how your program may have contributed to those results, regardless of whether it is an intended program outcome or student learning and development outcome. An example of a program discussing their contributions to survey findings can be found at http://www.ncsu.edu/undergrad_affairs/assessment/files/projects/nsse/nsse_results_nso_program.pdf.

Identify negative aspects reported by the data. Describe how your program may have contributed to those results, regardless of whether it is an intended program outcome or student learning and development outcome. Then, determine ways in which you can identify decisions to improve those aspects.

Many times, surveys point you towards areas in which you are doing well or areas that need improvement, but they may not give you the detail you need to make the specific decisions for continuous improvement. Thus, when reviewing survey data, you may want to use the information to inform more detailed investigations of specific outcomes, in order to unearth information that will help you make decisions for continuous improvement.

If you need help in organizing and interpreting your mountains of data, get it. It may be that a faculty member on your campus is looking for such a project. In addition, you may be able to convince a graduate student or undergraduate student that assisting you with organizing, analyzing, and interpreting your data is the perfect project for their educational needs (Table 12–1). It is often a good idea to analyze and interpret all the survey data that your institution has prior to your selection of another survey and prior to the planning of your timetable. Also, consult Table 12–2 for cost-saving tips.

TABLE 12–1

Students Can Assist You with Survey Research

Students can

- assist with the design of surveys through review of literature, choosing pop language over academic language when appropriate, identifying the arrangement of most important aspects of the survey, and pretesting the survey; and

- increase survey response through invitations by students to students.

TABLE 12–2

Cost-saving Tips

- Standardized surveys do not need to be administered every year. If you administer only when you feel you have had time to implement the improvement to the program (that resulted from an earlier survey administration) and then reassess, whether that be every other year or every four years, you will save money and maximize time commitment.

- Consider pooling interdepartmental and interdivision resources in order to make the administration and analysis of a standardized survey more affordable.

- Be sure you have analyzed and interpreted all the survey data that your institution has prior to your selection of another survey and prior to the planning of your timetable. Many institutions sit on mounds of data and do not analyze or interpret them or make decisions based on them. If left unattended, this is an obvious resource drain. Thus, if you thoroughly research what data your institution has collected prior to administering a new survey, you will benefit by making a more informed decision.

- Analyzing the data yourself may save you money or may cost you more money. Thoroughly research the data analysis options that accompany some instruments and determine which is the best value for your time.

- Partner with your academic colleagues. Many junior faculty (as well as some graduate and undergraduate students) are looking for research opportunities. You can capitalize on their research expertise and provide them access to data that they can use for publication and information, which you can use to inform decisions for continuous improvement.

CHAPTER 13

Portfolios

Using Portfolios to Assess Institutional Outcomes

If you have read this book from cover to cover, you have noted that there are many tools for you to examine when determining how to evaluate any given student learning and development outcome. You have learned what questions to ask and how to examine your outcome so that you know how best to proceed with its assessment. With portfolios, the challenge of choosing it as a tool to assess a particular outcome can be a little bit different. In order to illustrate, examine this definition of portfolios: Portfolios "are a type of assessment in which students' work is systematically collected and carefully reviewed for evidence of learning and development" (Palomba & Banta, 1999, p. 131).

In the aforementioned definition, the key word is "systematic." Portfolios are often thought of as a purposeful collection of artifacts to demonstrate a student's learning and development. Typically, the systematic approach means that throughout the student's academic career, there are specific data collection points for exact outcomes. The outcomes are usually those of the institution and reflect the institution's student learning principles or institutional competencies. Alverno College (http://ddp.alverno.edu/) has one of the most sophisticated examples of this type of student learning portfolio. Their outcomes include communication, analysis, problem solving, valuing, social interaction, effective citizenship, and aesthetic response (http://depts.alverno.edu/saal/).

While you may be wondering what this example has to do with academic and student support services' assessment of student learning and development, examine the outcomes more closely. Which of those outcomes does not express a value of one or more of your programs? If you see outcomes not reflected in your program, try

another example. San Diego Miramar College's (http://www.miramar.sdccd.net/projects/league/index.asp) draft of their 21st Century Learning Outcomes Project is asking all to assess the extent to which their graduates exhibit communication skills, critical thinking, problem solving, global awareness, information management, wellness, teamwork, conflict resolution, and personal responsibility. As cocurricular specialists, these are values you may espouse as well. One of the ways you can assess these outcomes is through student learning portfolios.

By systematically planning your program assessment, you can ask the students involved in your programs to demonstrate, through well-coordinated projects, their contributions to your institution's student learning principles. These student-learning principles may also be program outcomes you desire to assess. If you are not yet at this level of conversation at your institution, do not give up. Portfolios may still be a great way for you to assess your program or activity's contribution to student learning. So, before we tell you how to assess using portfolios or before you get discouraged because your institution is not ready to do this kind of assessment, let us tell you about another way you can use portfolio assessment (Table 13–1).

Using Portfolios to Assess Programs, Activities, or Specific Outcomes

Huba and Freed (2000) describe another type of portfolio—a portfolio where the student and cocurricular specialist evaluate a single outcome or set of outcomes related to each other. One specific example includes the assessment of a leadership program, which desires for *students to demonstrate 21st century leadership skills*. Since this is a large outcome, the program administrators have

TABLE 13-1

Examples of Portfolios

- Learning Careers Project and Folio Thinking from Stanford Center for Innovations in Learning— www.naspa.org/netresults/article.cfm?ID=825

- American Association for Higher Education (AAHE)— http://aahe.ital.utexas.edu/electronicportfolios/index.html

- Indiana University—Purdue University, Indianapolis— http://www.iport.iupui.edu/

- University of Minnesota—http://portfolio.umn.edu/

- Rose-Hulman Institute of Technology— http://www.rose-hulman.edu/irpa/reps/

- University of Wisconsin—Superior— http://www2.uwsuper.edu/assessment/

broken it down into several sub-outcomes, which then can be assessed over the student's academic year involvement in this program.

Each sub-outcome of *organizational skills, interpersonal relationships, ethics, problem solving, the ability to evaluate character, oral and written communication, application of organizational behavior theories,* and *personal responsibility* is assessed with an artifact in the portfolio using tools identified in the previous chapters. The portfolio then is a culmination of evidence such as presentations that have been made to student government; a Meyer's Briggs evaluation; an essay about the student's self-interpretation of his/her type; problem-solving case studies evaluated with a criteria checklist; a booklet demonstrating the student's organizational skills when he/she was chairing a Student Senate committee; standardized personality tests with the student's self-evaluation; and an essay describing an understanding of the decision-making process along with a rubric that was used to evaluate the essay, the student, and leadership. Program administrators use this collection of artifacts to evaluate the student's journey toward becoming a 21st century leader.

With this one example, you can see the wealth of information that is gathered for each of the leadership program outcomes and by the individual student. This type of evidence provides a great deal of information about what can be improved for each student and how. In

addition, this type of assessment can be both formative and summative (see Chapter Two), thus allowing for improvement decisions to be made throughout the administration of the program.

Similar to the example of asking students to create portfolios that demonstrate their individual learning of several outcomes espoused by one program is the development of a program portfolio where you, the cocurricular specialist, bring in sample work from the students with whom you work. As a recreational services cocurricular specialist in the following portfolio example, you are selecting samples of students' work to demonstrate that *students manage their personal health and well-being.* The students' work comes from the various ways in which you are assessing this outcome. In addition, you add other artifacts as to whether this outcome has been met. Your artifacts include:

- A random selection of the "one-minute paper" [1](Angelo & Cross, 1993, p. 148) assigned to first-year students after having completed your required health and wellness seminar.

- An observation of students in the recreation center, analyzed with a criteria checklist.

- A random selection of the answers to the intake form question you requested. (Last year, you asked your institutional health care practitioners to add a question to their intake form, which asks students how well they are managing their personal health and well-being.)

- A summary of the interviews of the health care workers to see if students are applying what they learned in the seminar to their daily lives.

These artifacts are gathered into your portfolio for this outcome and then analyzed in accordance with what you learned in Chapter Eleven, or you apply a criteria checklist or rubric (see Chapter Five) to see if you can identify evidence of that which you desired students to learn. If you can identify the evidence, you know what to keep doing with your seminars. If you cannot see any evidence, then you may know exactly what to change in your seminar or you may know what recommendations to make. Sharing your findings, decisions, and recommendations with those who helped you with gathering the data illustrates your commitment to helping them

---

[1] The "one-minute paper" consists of students writing their responses to the following questions: (1) What was the most important thing you learned?, and (2) What is one question you still have? (Cross & Angelo, 1993, p. 148).

with their work (for they may share the same outcome) and also proves how you could keep the information they shared with you in confidence and analyzed in a manner that students' identities were not at risk.

Here is another example from a student conduct office, where student portfolios are used to measure learning and development outcomes for students involved in the student judicial system. Specifically, portfolios are used to measure the following outcomes:

- Students that violate the Code will demonstrate insight into how their behavior affects all aspects of their life through a variety of writing assignments.

- Students that violate the Code will demonstrate improved decision-making skills through a variety of writing assignments.

- Students that violate the Code will demonstrate a change in behaviors.

When students are assigned a portfolio, they are asked to articulate personal goals and then gather evidence to demonstrate that they are working towards those goals. This exercise is designed to assist them in making intentional behavioral choices that are consistent with their goals. They then reflect on their evidence and goals and write a reflective paper about their experience. In the reflective paper, the student responds to a series of questions designed to elicit information about the outcomes and a rubric is used to determine if the student met the above outcomes. The rubric is based on literature on insight and decision-making skills. Whether you are assessing institutional outcomes or program outcomes, portfolios have significant benefits, uses, and purposes (Table 13–2).

TABLE 13–2

What is a Portfolio?

- Portfolios are a collection of artifacts to demonstrate that one has accomplished that which he/she said he/she would accomplish.

- Portfolios can be used to assess a student's learning and development, a program's accomplishments, an institution's accomplishments, or a professional's achievements.

- Portfolios can come in a variety of forms (e.g., paper, electronic, multi-media)

Benefits of Using Portfolios

While portfolios require significant planning and preparation, there are incredible benefits to this type of assessment (Table 13–3). For example,

- Portfolios provide the evaluator and the student with wonderful opportunities for reflection (Huba & Freed, 2000). However, portfolios require a great deal of planning to identify which outcomes will be assessed and which artifacts will be gathered for evaluation. In addition, decisions about which artifacts to include in the portfolio also need to be made. Furthermore, there could be other assessment tools added to evaluate artifacts along the planned portfolio timeline and possibly additional tools, such as rubrics to evaluate the portfolio for its overall learning outcomes. Such planning requires a great deal of reflection about what it is that you want students to learn, how you will go about providing them with those learning experiences, and how you will provide them with the opportunities to demonstrate that which they have learned.

- Portfolios provide opportunities for cocurricular specialists and academics to collaborate on delivering opportunities for learning (Maki, 2003). Because of the reflection and planning that is required to design and implement portfolios, a great deal of conversation and collaboration among faculty and cocurricular specialists is required. Consider not only the examples of collaborating to assess institutional learning principles, but also the coordination needed to plan assessment of analytical reasoning and critical thinking.

- Portfolios can feature multiple examples of context-rich work (Cambridge, 2001). As you have seen from the aforementioned examples, multiple artifacts can prove extremely beneficial to assessing student learning and development in several venues, thus providing program administrators as well as students with information about their own learning.

- Portfolios can offer opportunities for selection and self-assessment (Cambridge, 2001). One great advantage to portfolio assessment is the role that students play in their own assessment. If you create an outcome as general as *demonstrate leadership or communication skills,* students could be asked to provide artifacts that they think best illustrate their learning and achievements in these areas. If provided with a rubric, they can evaluate their own progress and possibly provide you with additional artifacts, as well as improvements to the rubric, particularly if their learning style is prohibiting them from providing evidence of their learning given your request.

- Portfolios provide students an opportunity to see the interrelatedness of many of their work assignments (Huba & Freed, 2000). If cocurricular specialists collaborate on designing a portfolio to assess shared outcomes such as communications skills, conflict resolution, problem solving, wellness, and ability to manage change, then students begin to connect the experiences they have in one program to another.

- Portfolios can offer a look at development over time (Cambridge, 2001). Another advantage to portfolios is that they can provide students with a look at their progress in any given outcome over time, as well as prior to and after specific experiences. Consider the outcome of civic engagement. Students can place in their portfolio a self-report civic engagement tool and reflection essays prior to their service-learning experience. After their service experience, they could complete the same tools, evaluate them, and see for themselves how they may have grown in their thinking and application of the principles they learned. If students have an opportunity to document their learning through portfolios over a longer period of time, they will see even greater learning and development.

- Portfolios may assess the value added by the institutional experience, but not necessarily the value added by the program. Throughout this book, we have been addressing assessment as a means to gather information in order to make decisions for continuous improvement. If students begin their portfolio assessment of the institutional learning principles as first-year students, the gathering of evidence over their academic career will prove beneficial to all constituents understanding how and what the students learned as a result of their cumulative academic career. Trying to decide which academic or cocurricular program was exclusively responsible for specific learning is a little more challenging and, hopefully, not necessary.

- Portfolios provide students with an understanding of how they learn (Alverno College Faculty, 1999). If portfolios are used to evaluate several learning and development outcomes over time and students have a role in their own self-evaluation, students will begin to better understand how they learn and, thus, possibly become more responsible for their own learning and development. Having students take responsibility for their learning is an outcome valued by cocurricular and curricular specialists.

TABLE 13–3

Simple Steps to Creating a Portfolio

- Choose the outcome(s) you wish to assess using the portfolios.
- Choose the type of portfolio you want to use (e.g., institutional, program, or outcome-specific).
- Choose the format of the portfolio (e.g., electronic or paper).
- Choose the artifacts that will be placed in the portfolio— make sure they will provide evidence of whether the chosen outcome(s) has (have) been met.
- Coordinate the gathering of artifacts with students and your cocurricular and faculty colleagues.
- Decide if you will be selecting work from all students or if you will be using a random sample or other type of sample (e.g., purposeful, best-case/worse-case).
- Decide how you will analyze the portfolio.
- Decide how you will report the information gathered and decisions made from the portfolio.

Questions to Ask When Developing a Portfolio
(Adapted from Huba & Freed, 2000, p. 264)

In addition to the assessment planning questions posed in Chapter Two, following is a list of questions to consider when using portfolios as an assessment tool:

- What is the primary purpose of using portfolios? Is it to evaluate student learning in a program or to promote and support individual student learning directly?

- What intended learning outcomes would your portfolio be evaluating?

- Do you plan to be a part of the student's portfolio that is assessing institutional outcomes, or do you plan to organize portfolio assessment for your own program or for individual outcomes in your program?

- What will the role of the cocurricular specialists be in evaluating the portfolios?

- What will the role of the students be in evaluating the portfolios?

- Will students select the artifacts to be included in their portfolio, or will you choose those for them?

- If you select the artifacts for the student portfolio, what will you select? And how do these artifacts show evidence of the desired student learning and development?

- If you are designing a program portfolio, will you use samples from all students in your program; or will you use a random selection, purposeful sample, or a best-case and worst-case selection?

- In what form will the portfolios be captured, and where will they be housed: on paper in a file cabinet or box, on a folder on the program's server, on the web, on a CD or disc, or in a database?

- Who will organize the instructions for the portfolio?

- Who will compile the student's work into the portfolios?

- Who will organize the gathering of the other types of evidence for the portfolio, should you choose other types of evidence?

- Who will maintain the portfolios?

- How will they be archived: on a CD, server, or scanned and stored on microfilm?

- Will the portfolios be considered public documents? If so, how will you protect students' privacy?

- When, how often, and by whom will the portfolios be reviewed?

- How will you disseminate findings from the portfolio reviews?

Analyzing and Reporting Information Gathered from a Portfolio

As you can see, analyzing the evidence contained in portfolios is not simply a matter of choosing an analytical tool. While in some cases it may be that simple, it is dependent on what types of evidence you have gathered and how you want to use that information to make decisions for continuous improvement.

Most users of portfolios construct a rubric (see Chapter Five) to evaluate the entire portfolio contents. And similar to the reporting options for rubrics, users will either summarize their findings, decisions, and recommendations in a narrative or report percentages of successfully learned skills and competencies (see Chapter Five). As mentioned previously, Alverno College has enhanced students' abilities to take responsibility for their own learning by providing them with a key role in their self-evaluation of their learning portfolio. While we will not be able to do justice to their decades of exemplary work nor will we be able to explain in detail how effective self-assessment works, you can learn more about self-assessment from the Alverno College Faculty (1999) book entitled, *Self-Assessment at Alverno College*. Huba and Freed's (2000) book on *Learner-Centered Assessment on College Campuses* is also an excellent resource. See http://depts.alverno.edu/saal/saframe.html for an illustration of the strength of student self-assessment in Alverno College's work. Finally, there are rubrics and criteria available for analyzing the structure of portfolios (Table 13–4).

TABLE 13–4

Analyzing the Structure of Portfolios
(Source: Palomba & Banta, 1999, p. 140.)

Criteria	Rating Scale	Score
Organization	3 = Has clear framework	
	2 = Framework present, but lacks clarity	
	1 = Framework not apparent	
Completeness	3 = All elements present	
	2 = Most items present	
	1 = Several items missing	

Evaluating your portfolios using the aforementioned criteria contributes to your understanding of how well-organized portfolios can be used efficiently for assessing student work. Analyzing the structure of portfolios may be helpful to you in order to determine the usefulness of portfolios. However, once you become confident in your ability to use portfolios to evaluate student learning, we believe you may find more value in using your analysis time on whether your outcomes for student learning and development have been met, rather than whether the structure of your portfolios is sound (Tables 13–5 and 13–6).

TABLE 13–5

Cost-saving Tips

- Portfolios are not inexpensive to use. If you choose an electronic format, the technological infrastructure can be costly, yet vendors are increasingly providing solutions. The ones we are aware of are presented at the end of this chapter. It is important when choosing an electronic solution to be mindful that you are making an investment in an effective way of reflecting and improving student learning.

- While the use of paper portfolios may appear to be the least expensive, the cost is higher in time invested, as you literally need to hand portfolio documents from one cocurricular specialist to another. In addition, sometimes there is a cost for copies.

- An inexpensive alternative may be to use a shared server in which you file the portfolios electronically. While you have to work through security access issues, and while it may be a bit cumbersome at times, it is a cheaper alternative than web-based portfolios.

- If you can financially manage the investment, we highly recommend web-based portfolios. The benefits of multiple secure access means more cocurricular specialists and faculty can interact with students as they learn more about what students know and can do.

TABLE 13–6

Electronic Portfolio Websites

- AAHE–http://aahe.ital.utexas.edu/electronicportfolios/index.html
- Indiana University–Purdue University, Indianapolis–http://www.iport.iupui.edu/
- Using Technology to Support Alternative Assessment and Electronic Portfolios–http://transition.alaska.edu/www/portfolios.html
- The Portfolio Clearinghouse–http://www.aahe.org/teaching/portfolio_db.htm
- Electronic Portfolios–http://www.essdack.org/port/
- TracDAT–www.nuventive.com
- WebFolio–www.iwebfolio.com
- Eportaro–http://www.eportaro.com/
- SAS–www.sas.com

CHAPTER 14

Documenting Assessment Findings and Decisions

The Issue

The actual steps of engaging in assessment are not new to many higher education faculty and administrators. Oftentimes, it is the terminology used in assessment that is new. Furthermore, assessment is not typically implemented in a systematic way (Maki, 2001; Banta, Black, & Kline, 2001; Anderson, 2001a, 2001b), which would result in documented outcomes, findings, and decisions made from those findings. Thus, when individuals attempt to demonstrate that they have engaged in assessment by articulating outcomes, gathering data to measure those outcomes, and making decisions for continuous improvement, there is no evidence to reveal.

As we previously discussed, the lack of evidence may be because the cocurricular specialist has not done the work of assessment; however, it may be because there is no evidence that assessment has been completed. There is no evidence because none of the steps in the process were documented—in any manner. So, why should assessment be documented? This chapter will illustrate why providing documentation of the assessment process is important not just for accountability, but also for learning even more about how well a program or course meets the intended end result.

The Introduction

Why do we have to be able to present evidence that we are engaged in assessment? Isn't it enough to go about the process of assessment so that improvements in education can be made? You have heard this argument before, and we once answered the latter question with a resounding "yes." As a matter of fact, it was not until we started reading the works of assessment experts that we realized we were engaged in assessment but were not familiar with the terminology, nor did we understand

the systematic process that should accompany assessment. It was in reading about the systematic process of assessment that we realized documentation is a necessary part of the entire process.

One reason to document the assessment process—and one that we are all aware of—is that higher education, in all its aspects, is undergoing increased scrutiny (Upcraft & Schuh, 1996). One only needs to pick up a local newspaper to read of how the public does not understand why "x" was spent on "y," why there needs to be a transition program for any given population, and why newly hired graduates cannot follow simple directions in their new task. Higher education undergoes increasing inspection about the learning it can produce (Ewell, 2002); yet, we still refuse to understand why we have to document the intended results of that which we do. Until now, we have been able to survive on our own beliefs, traditions, and our rich institutional history, which included our own undocumented assessment of our work.

We are now at an age of increased accountability. We need to document the effectiveness, or lack thereof, for all of our constituents. Accountability is what we most often hear as the reason as to why we should document our assessment process. It is logical and obvious. Yet, many cocurricular professionals and faculty are still not documenting their work (Anderson, 2001a, 2001b).

While documenting the assessment process has had great benefits in the accountability and budget arenas, the true reward for us was in learning more about our programs (Maki, 2003). Simply put, we have learned more about our programs and courses because we had to document the assessment process. We believe that we need to go through the process of documenting our own assessment work for ourselves, as well as for the direct benefactors of our programs and classes. What do we mean? We will attempt to illustrate this point with a personal example from one of the author's courses.

The Example: One of Marilee Bresciani's Courses

When we first began to get serious about assessment, we approached it with a bit of arrogance. How hard could this be?, we asked. We believed assessment was common sense, and we felt we had been doing it for years—at least the part where we asked if the program had produced what we expected upon its completion and why or why not. We even administered satisfaction questionnaires to program participants and used that information, along with our observations, to make improvements in the next cycle. Throughout this process of asking if the program "worked," we never took the time to document the intended outcomes of the program prior to the start of the program. Nor did we record the findings in a manner that could tie to any sort of outcomes. Furthermore, we did not write down the decisions we made to improve the program. We did not even document and celebrate program successes. No one even asked us for the information. We just made changes in each program cycle.

It was not until we started to attempt to record the entire process that we realized the documentation process itself provided incredible learning opportunities about how our programs or courses worked. Writing down what it was that we wanted a program or a course to accomplish (e.g., what learning and development we wanted to see in the students and participants), before we even delivered the program or course, caused great reflection as to why we were even offering the program or the course. For example, when I taught an enrollment management course, one of the learning outcomes was that the *students would be able to interpret financial aid yield analysis in order to determine how to influence yield through the controllable aspects of their institution's financial aid.* In articulating this as an outcome, I had to ask myself why I thought this was an important outcome, given all that students need to learn about enrollment management. I had an answer, and the answer resulted in a refinement of this outcome, allowing me to use the classroom and assignment time in a more productive manner.

Implementing the Outcome

There was still more learning for me in the articulation of an outcome. After articulating the aforementioned outcome, I realized that in the course I had offered in

the past, there was no learning component for students to understand what portions of a financial aid package could be influenced by their institution so that they could then learn what aid could be adjusted in order to attempt to influence yield. I had other learning opportunities for students for the other steps that led to the fulfillment of this outcome, but I had missed this very important piece. Articulating this outcome and changing the course syllabus saved the students and me from unnecessary frustrations during the course. In addition, just writing this assessment process down helped me to ensure that I would better meet this particular outcome.

Recording the Assessment Methods

As I continued in the assessment planning and the recording of each assessment step, I realized that I was not giving students any opportunity to demonstrate that they had learned how to interpret the financial aid yield analysis. I was not providing an opportunity for students to demonstrate the application of this information in their final project. Furthermore, I was missing an opportunity to check the students' understanding of this aspect after the portion of this learning had occurred or was supposed to occur. It was not until I tried to document where I would gather evidence for this outcome that this realization occurred. I now understood that I had no opportunity to capture the evidence in place, yet since this realization occurred during the assessment planning, I had time to implement the remedy, and I did.

In documenting how I would measure each outcome, I also discovered that some of the methods I had used in the past were not really gathering evidence for any outcome. Instead, I was gathering evidence that the students were satisfied with how the group projects were presented or that they liked my *PowerPoint* slides. Neither piece of evidence gave me too much information about what the students were learning; all I knew was that they liked the group projects and the slides. Interesting information, but I could save the students and me time by asking questions that were going to provide me with more meaningful information on which to improve my course. Thus, I could improve my assessment efforts by reallocating time from earlier efforts that were less productive.

Recording the Findings

As you may know from your own experiences, it is one thing to look at data and make decisions, and quite another to commit to writing down one's interpretation of the data. Recording the findings from our assessment methods as they relate to whether an outcome had been achieved provided us with two learning opportunities. One was in the viewing of the data and the consideration of how well the chosen assessment method measured the outcome. This documentation step provided us with opportunities to improve the assessment method, the implementation of the outcome, and the articulation of the outcome itself.

The other learning came in gauging the extent to which the outcome was assessed and met. In recording the findings, we had visibly committed ourselves to making a decision to improve, in knowing that something either had gone really well or not so well. In this step, we felt we were saying to the world, now we know the end result and now we need to do something about it. The first time we set out to write down our first assessment finding, we literally felt afraid. For some reason, we felt that writing the results down made us more vulnerable, as if someone would see our inner faults and blame us for being a bad teacher or program administrator. Now, the documenting comes with much less fear and much more liberation as we find this step helpful in simply reminding us of what we need to change the next go around and exactly why.

Recording the Decisions Made

The final step is the process of recording the decision that was made. (And yes, maintaining the status quo is a decision and in this day and age of tightening institutional budgets; it is not necessarily an easy one to make.) Again, as you know, most of us do make decisions based on our assessment results, but we just may not write them down. Why should we? Well, of course, to demonstrate accountability—that we did something with the information we collected. Recording decisions may also serve as helpful reminders to ourselves and to others about why we made the decision(s) we did. (Don't laugh too hard! We need all the reminders we can get.) For example, with tightening budgets, I am able to only teach the enrollment management course once every three or four years. This time frame requires a dramatic update in the course readings and assignments. This time frame also means that I cannot remember the assessment outcomes of the previous course and the decisions I made to improve that course when I teach it next time, unless I write them down. If this example sounds weak, let us pose another.

A few weeks ago we had our program retreat so that we could review our assessment findings, outcomes, and record interpretation of results and decisions made. As we poured through the assessment plan and the data, a previous year's particular outcome, findings, and decision struck us. Just moments before seeing this "decision," we had made a sarcastic comment about the "idiot" who attempted to assess the outcome of a particular program without going back to check and see if the participants even understood the overall concept. Well, you can probably guess who the idiot was—it was I (Marilee speaking here). Having recorded the decision made, though, reminded us that there had been no time for that particular "check;" and we had recorded some of what we thought, of course, were pretty good reminders so that we would not make that mistake again. Not only could we not remember that had happened, but also we could not have remembered the recommendations that we made in the midst of it all to ensure we would not repeat that error.

Now, while we may have convinced you that we are the most absent-minded people alive, we hope that we have made a little bit of sense regarding the value to you of documenting your assessment work. If you are still reading this, then you may be interested in learning about various ways of documenting your assessment process. We do not know of any wrong way to do this. If you have discovered a wrong way, please let us know so we can avoid it and tell others to do the same. Following are some methods of documentation. All of them vary in benefits and time committed to that particular process.

Ways to Document Assessment Processes

There are several ways to document the assessment process; decide which method works most effectively for you. For example,

- Word processing programs
- Spreadsheets
- Relational databases
- Diagrams
- Web
- Videotape
- Audiotape

Political Challenges

The political challenges of documenting and sharing evidence and decisions made based on assessment findings are topics for another book. It may very well be that the documentation of your assessment process is too political to share with anyone, let alone your colleagues. It is true that when we attempt to find information about how well our students learn as a result of our program, we find information about another's program. Thus, while we may desire transparency in our process, our colleagues may not. Strategies to address these kinds of challenges vary by institution, but strategies do exist. These strategies are truly a topic for another chapter.

Conclusion

Documenting the assessment process is valuable for demonstrating accountability and for personal learning about one's program and course outcomes. There are several ways in which to document the process; no one is more "right" than the other. There is, however, no way around the time that it takes to record assessment plans and results in a meaningful way. Time is a valuable commodity, and it is needed in order to make this all work. We continue to hope that more will see the value of investing the time in meaningful and manageable assessment, which requires documenting the process. And it is our hope that the investment in assessment will pay off unimaginable dividends.

Thus, we invite you to share with us your program improvements made by using assessment. Write to us and tell us about what you have learned through assessment. We would love to feature your work in NASPA's *NetResults* and encourage you to share them with others. You can send us your documentation by e-mailing Marilee_Bresciani@ncsu.edu or by sending your work to Marilee Bresciani, North Carolina State University, Division of Undergraduate Affairs, Office of Assessment, CB #7105, Raleigh, NC 27713-7105.

APPENDIX A

College/Department/Unit Assessment Diversity and Student, Staff, and Faculty Success

Guidelines: The attached guidelines provide a framework for a holistic and balanced diagnosis of the organization. This assessment should specifically address issues of diversity and student, staff, and faculty success. These guidelines will help an organization focus on the dimensions and actions that contribute to achieving results and will include planning, execution of plans, assessment of progress, and cycles of improvement. These criteria are also nonprescriptive and allow each organization to address their individual character and unique issues and needs without being limited to set practices or specific approaches to achieve the desired results. The questions are intentionally broad and ask for a focused response in three dimension: (1) the approach—one that is systematic, integrated and consistently applied; (2) the deployment—the extent to which the approach is applied; and (3) results—the measures of performance and success relative to appropriate comparisons.

Scoring: Each area should be assessed using the attached scoring guidelines. These guidelines will determine the levels of maturity of the approach, deployment, and results within the organization.

Organizational Overview: Before completing this assessment, it would be beneficial for the leadership team to prepare an outline that will identify the characteristics and issues that are unique, relevant, and important to the organization. This will allow each organization flexibility in selecting an approach consistent with given circumstances. It will also allow the organization to define a set of valid measures of success for each population.

Basic Description: Provide a mission description, the profile of the organization's populations, and the nature of the organization's programs and activities.

Stakeholder/Constituent Requirements: Identify the important stakeholders and their requirements to include specific programs, activities, and services.

Partnerships: Identify special partnership arrangements and their special requirements (if any).

Performance: Identify the principal factors that determine performance success and the performance leaders in similar organizations.

Other Factors: Provide information that describes the unique nature of the organization, new developments, or factors that affect.

Leadership: Describe how leaders provide effective leadership in fostering diversity and success within the organization, taking into account the needs and expectations of all key stakeholders

- How does the leadership team communicate and clearly incorporate the values of diversity and student, faculty, and staff success in the organization's directions and expectations?

- How does the leadership team communicate the expectations for accountability throughout the organization?

- How does the leadership team seek future opportunities to incorporate and embed the values of diversity and success in the organization?

- How does the leadership team maintain a climate conducive to learning, equity, and success?

84

- How does the leadership team incorporate the views and efforts of all constituencies (underrepresented and majority) into the leadership system?

Organizational Strategy: Describe how the organization sets strategic direction and how this strategy is translated into action plans and performance requirements

- How are implementation responsibilities decided and assigned?

- How does the organization track organizational performance relative to the plans?

- How are process barriers (that impede progress) identified and incorporated into the strategic plans and actions?

Stakeholder Knowledge/Focus: Describe how the organization determines the requirements and expectations of students, staff, faculty, and other important constituents relative to satisfaction, support, and success

- How does the organization listen and learn from its faculty, staff, students, and other important constituents?

- How are key programs, activities, and services determined or projected into the future?

- How are the relative importance/value of programs, activities, and services determined or projected into the future?

- How are constituent inputs, including retention and complaints, used to improve organizational performance?

Selection and Use of Data and Information: Describe the organization's selection, management, and use of data and information needed to support key processes and to improve organization performance

- What are the main types of data and information (e.g., instructional, operations and constituent data), and how does each relate and align to the diversity and success goals?

- How are the data and information integrated into the measurements that can be used to track and improve the organization's performance and success?

Education, Training, and Development: Describe how the organization's education and training address key organization plans and needs, including building knowledge and capabilities and contributing to improved performance, diversity, development, and success

- How do education and training address the key performance plans and needs, including longer-term employee development?

- How are the education and training designed and delivered?

- How are knowledge and skills reinforced on the job?

Education and Support Processes: Describe how the organization's key processes (educational and support) are designed, managed, and improved to incorporate the themes of diversity and success

- How are key requirements determined or set? (Incorporate inputs from appropriate constituents.)

- How are key educational and support process designed to meet the overall current and future performance requirements?

- How are the processes managed to maintain process performance and to ensure results will meet the requirements and desired outcomes?

Results: Summarize the results of diversity and measures of success using key measures or indicators of educational and support performance

- Summarize current levels and trends in key measures or indicators of performance. Include comparative data (internal or national benchmarks). These measures should include regulatory/legal compliance, as well as others that support the organization's strategy (e.g., new programs or services).

Self-Assessment Scoring Guidelines

Stage 1: Beginning

- There is no systematic approach to respond to the criteria

- Information is anecdotal in nature

- Early stages of gathering data, little to no trend data

- The approach is confined to senior management

Stage 2: Development

- There is the beginning of a systematic approach to address the issues

- The organization is in the early stages of transition from reacting to problems to the early stages of anticipating issues

- Major gaps exist that inhibit progress in achieving the intent of the criteria

- The beginning of a fact-based approach is evident

- Beginning stages of improvement cycles

- The approach extends beyond the senior management

- Little to no comparative data

Stage 3: Sound

- A sound and systematic approach is evident and responsive to the primary purpose of the criteria

- A fact-based improvement process is in place in key areas

- More emphasis is placed on improving rather than reacting to problems

- Improvement trends or good performance reported in many to most areas

- Organization has comparative data in most key areas

Stage 4: Mature

- A sound and systematic approach responsive to the overall purposes of the criteria

- A fact-based improvements process is a key management tool and clear evidence of cycles of refinement and improvement analysis

- The approach is well-deployed throughout the organization

- Current performance is excellent in most areas with excellent trends

- Organization uses comparative data in all areas and leads or competes favorably in the key areas

APPENDIX B

Oral Presentation Rubric

Presenter's Name: _____

	Distinguished	Intermediate	Novice
Volume	Presenter is easy to hear. 10	"Audience is able to hear as a whole, but there are times when volume is not quite adequate. " 10	Presenter is difficult to hear. 5	0
Rates	Rates of speech are appropriate. 10	Speaker may at times seem like he/she is rushing or exaggerating pauses. 10	The rates of speaking are too slow or too fast. 5	0
Mannerisms	Speaker makes eye contact with everyone and has no nervous habits. Speaker has excellent posture. 10	Eye contact may focus on only one member of the audience or a select few members. Mildly distracting nervous habits are present but do not override the content. 10	Very little eye contact is made with the audience. It may sound like the speaker is reading the presentation. Nervous habits that distract the audience are present. 5	0
Engagement	Presentation involves audience, allowing time for audience to think and respond. 10	Audience is involved but inadequate processing or response time is provided. 10	Speaker does not involve audience. 5	0
Organization	Presentation is well organized with a beginning, middle, and end. There is a strong organizing theme, with clear main ideas and transitions. 20	Speaker loses train of thought, does not stay with the proposed outline, or connections are attempted but not made clear for the audience. 20	Presentation shows little organization, unclear purpose, or unclear relationships or transitions. " 10	0
Content	Information is complete and accurate. Clear evidence of research. 20	Research component is less evident than in distinguished category, or resources are present but less than adequate for assignment. 20	Details and examples are lacking or not well chosen for the topic or audience. Lacks evidence of research. 10	0
Visual Aids/ Handouts	Visual aids are well done and are used to make presentation more interesting and meaningful. 10	Visuals are adequate but do not inspire engagement with the material. 10	Very little or poor use of visual materials. No handouts provided. 5	0
Length	Appropriate length. Clear summary is provided. Audience is involved in synthesizing the information. 10	Time is appropriately used, but may run slightly over or under allotted time or information is not tied together or conclusion is inadequate. 10	Presentation lacks conclusion or time is not appropriately used. 5	0

Comments:

"Bresciani and Bowman, 2002"

APPENDIX C

Diversity Project Selection Checklist

The following checklist may be used as a guide for selecting a diversity project. It cannot be assumed that everyone is at the same starting place both in terms of motivation and readiness. Projects that satisfy an increasing number of criteria on the checklist inspire more confidence. If only a **limited** number of items can be checked off about the project, you may want to revaluate your choice.

____ 1- The diversity project is related to basic campus issues as opposed to narrow or isolated ones.

____ 2- The diversity project has direct impact upon some targeted group. (This is especially important for short-term projects or projects early in a diversity improvement effort.)

____ 3- The diversity project has broad visibility on campus.

____ 4- All persons who will be asked to implement the diversity project, at all levels, agree that it is important to initiate the project.

____ 5- The diversity project can be evaluated periodically.

____ 6- The diversity project involves a broad range of participants.

____ 7- The diversity project involves a clearly defined process that has easily-identified starting and ending points.

____ 8- The diversity project does not overextend projected costs and available resources.

____ 9- The diversity project reflects some part of the existing mission statement and the dominant values of a campus.

____ 10- The diversity project has a sound conceptual framework that can be identified and explained as an asset to a campus.

APPENDIX D

EAC 779: Course Evaluation

Please complete this evaluation and return to <u>Marilee_Bresciani@ncsu.edu</u>; fax to 919-515-4416; or mail to North Carolina State University, Division of Undergraduate Affairs, 126 Leazar Hall, CB#7105, Raleigh, North Carolina, 27695-7105. Your comments will be used to make informed decisions for the improvement of this course. Thank you.

Section I:

Using the following scale (1=strongly disagree, 2= disagree, 3= neutral, 4=agree, 5= strongly agree), please circle the number that is most representative of your level of agreement with each statement.

	Strongly Disagree				**Strongly Agree**
1. This course helped me better understand evaluation and assessment concepts.	1	2	3	4	5
2. This course helped me better understand issues used in educational evaluation.	1	2	3	4	5
3. This course helped me better understand models used in educational evaluation.	1	2	3	4	5
4. This course helped me better articulate an understanding of the purpose for evaluation and assessment.	1	2	3	4	5
5. This course helped me better demonstrate the ability to plan evaluations for my program.	1	2	3	4	5
6. This course helped me better critique evaluation designs in order to determine possible reservations regarding use of reported findings.	1	2	3	4	5
7. This course helped me better identify various research, evaluation, and assessment challenges in higher education.	1	2	3	4	5
8. This course helped me better understand ethical issues intertwined in educational evaluation.	1	2	3	4	5
9. This course helped me better understand the purpose of assessment.	1	2	3	4	5
10. This course helped me better understand the benefits of assessment.	1	2	3	4	5

	Strongly Disagree				Strongly Agree
11. I will be able to apply what I learned in this course in my daily life.	1	2	3	4	5
12. I enjoyed this course.	1	2	3	4	5
13. The group exercises increased my understanding of the subject matter.	1	2	3	4	5
14. The student presentations increased my understanding of the subject matter.	1	2	3	4	5
15. The textbook readings increased my understanding of the subject matter.	1	2	3	4	5
16. The journal assignments increased my understanding of the subject matter.	1	2	3	4	5
17. The final project increased my understanding of the subject matter.	1	2	3	4	5
18. The instructor demonstrated evidence of expertise in the subject matter.	1	2	3	4	5
19. The instructor provided an environment where I felt free to ask questions.	1	2	3	4	5
20. The instructor provided me with ample opportunities to demonstrate my expertise in the subject matter.	1	2	3	4	5
21. I would recommend this course to another colleague.	1	2	3	4	5
22. I plan to utilize surveys to evaluate something in my work place.	1	2	3	4	5
23. I plan to utilize rubrics to evaluate something in my work place.	1	2	3	4	5
24. I plan to utilize interviews to evaluate something in my work place.	1	2	3	4	5
25. There is only one way to do assessment well.	1	2	3	4	5

Section II:

1) What was the most valuable lesson learned from this course?

2) What was the greatest strength of this course?

3) What would you change about this course?

4) What would you change about the instruction of the course?

5) What would have motivated you to learn more about the course content?

6) What is one question you still have about the course content?

7) Other comments:

REFERENCES

Allen, J., & Bresciani, M. J. (2003, January/February). Public institutions, public challenges: On the transparency of assessment results. *Change Magazine, 35* (1). Washington, D.C.: American Association for Higher Education.

Alverno College Faculty. (1999). *Self assessment at Alverno College.* Milwaukee, WI: Alverno College Institute.

American Association for Higher Education. (1994). *Nine principles of good practice for assessing student learning* [Online]. Retrieved from http://www.aahe.org/assessment/principl.htm

American College Personnel Association. (1994). *Student learning imperative: Implications for student affairs.* Washington, D.C.: Author.

Anderson, J. A. (2001a). Why assessment is important to student affairs. *NetResults* [Online]. Retrieved from http://www.naspa.org/

Anderson, J. A. (2001b). *Assessing what you value.* Presentation to the Division of Student Affairs at North Carolina State University, Raleigh, NC.

Andrade, H. G. (2000, February). Using rubrics to promote thinking and learning. *Educational Leadership, 57* (5).

Angelo, T., & Cross, K. P. (1993). Classroom assessment techniques: A handbook for college teachers (2nd ed.). San Francisco: Jossey-Bass.

Astin, A. (1996). Involvement in learning revisited: Lessons we have learned. *Journal of College Student Development, 37* (2), 132.

Babbie, E. (1990). *Survey research methods* (2nd ed.). Belmont, CA: Wadsworth Publishing.

Banta, T. W., Black, K. E., & Kline, K. A. (2001). The challenge to assess outcomes in student affairs. *NetResults* [Online]. Retrieved from http://www.naspa.org/

Barbazette, J. (2003). *Instant case studies for successful trainers: Adapt, use, and create your own case studies.* San Francisco: Pfeiffer.

Beauchamp, M., Parsons, J., & Sanford, K. (1996). Teaching from the outside in. *Duval, 37* [Online]. Retrieved from http://www.2learn.ca/projects/together/ START/rubricc.html

Berg, B. L. (2001). *Qualitative research methods for the social sciences* (4th ed.). Boston: Allyn and Bacon.

Bloom, B. S. (Ed.). (1956). *Taxonomy of education objectives: The classification of educational goal* (Handbook I, cognitive domain). New York: Longmans.

Bogdan, R. C., & Biklen, S. K. (1998). *Qualitative research for education: An introduction to theory and methods.* Boston: Allyn and Bacon.

Bresciani, M. J. (2001). Writing measurable and meaningful outcomes. *NetResults* [Online]. Retrieved from http://www.naspa.org/

Bresciani, M. J. (2002). Outcomes assessment in student affairs: Moving beyond satisfaction to student learning and development. *NetResults* [Online]. Retrieved from http://www.naspa.org/

Bresciani, M. J. (2003a). Creating a culture of assessment: Making assessment meaningful and manageable. *NetResults* [Online]. Retrieved from http://www.naspa.org/

Bresciani, M. J. (2003b). An updated outline for assessment plans. *NetResults* [Online]. Retrieved from http://www.naspa.org/

Cambridge, B. (Ed.) (2001). *Electronic portfolios: Emerging practices in student, faculty, and institutional learning.* Washington, D.C.: American Association of Higher Education.

Campbell, D. M., Melenyzer, B. J., Nettles, D. H., & Wyman, R. M. (2000). *Portfolio and performance assessment in teacher education.* Boston: Allyn and Bacon.

Center for Postsecondary Research & Planning, Indiana University. (2003). National Survey of Student Engagement [Online]. Retrieved from http://www.iub.edu/%7Ensse/

Cooperative Institutional Research Program Freshman Survey. (2003). [Online]. Retrieved from http://www.gseis.ucla.edu/heri/cirp.html

Cornell Critical Thinking Test [Online]. (2003). Retrieved from http://www.uttyler.edu/epp/cornell.htm

Deming, W. E. (1986). *Out of the crisis.* Cambridge, MA: Massachusetts Institute of Technology Center for Advanced Engineering.

Educational Benchmarking Incorporated [Online]. (2003). Retrieved from http://www.webebi.com/AboutEBI/Index.htm)

Educational Resources Information Center Clearing House on Higher Education. (2000). *Survey on the picture of curricular and co-curricular collaborations.* Washington, D.C.: American College Personnel Association and National Association of Student Personnel Administrators.

Engineering Communication Centre. (2002). Writing case studies [Online]. Retrieved from http://www.ecf.utoronto.ca/~writing/handbook-casestudies.html

Ewell, P. T. (1985). Some implications for practice. In P.T. Ewell (Ed.), *Assessing education outcomes* (New Directions for Institutional Research, no.47). San Francisco: Jossey-Bass.

Ewell, P. T. (1991). To capture the ineffable: New forms of assessment in higher education. In G. Grant (Ed.), *Review of research in education* (New Directions for Institutional Research, no.47). Washington D.C.: American Education Research Association.

Ewell, P. T. (1994). *A policy guide for assessment: Making good use of tasks in critical thinking.* Princeton, N.J.: Educational Testing Service.

Ewell, P. T. (1997a). From the states: Putting it all on the line—South Carolina's performance funding initiative. *Assessment Update, 9 (1),* 9, 11.

Ewell, P. T. (1997b). Identifying indicators of curricular quality. In G. J. Gaff, L. J. Ratcliff and Associates, *Handbook of the undergraduate curriculum: A comprehensive guide to purposes, structures, practices, and change.* San Francisco: Jossey-Bass.

Ewell, P. T. (2002). *Grading student learning: You have to start somewhere* [Online]. Retrieved from http://measuringup.highereducation.org/2002/articles/peterewell.htm

Gardiner, L. F. (1996). Redesigning higher education: Producing dramatic gains in student learning. *ASHE-ERIC Higher Education Report, 23* (7). Washington, D.C: The George Washington University, School of Education and Human Development.

Glesne, C. (1999). *Becoming qualitative researchers: An introduction* (2nd ed). New York: Longman.

Hanson, G., and Bresciani, M. J. (2003). *Advanced assessment workshop for student affairs professionals.* Washington, D.C.: National Association of Student Personnel Administrators.

Huba, M. E., and Freed, J. E. (2000). *Learner-centered assessment on college campuses: Shifting the focus from teaching to learning.* Boston: Allyn and Bacon.

Insight Assessment. (2003). California Critical Thinking Disposition Inventory [Online]. Retrieved from http://www.insightassessment.com/test-cctdi.html

Insight Assessment. (2003). California Critical Thinking Skills Test [Online]. Retrieved from http://www.insightassessment.com/tests.html

Joint Task Force on Student Learning. (1998). *Powerful partnerships: A shared responsibility for learning.* Washington, D.C.: National Association of Student Personnel Administrators.

Kezar, A. (2001). Documenting the landscape: Results of a national study on academic and student affairs collaborations. In *Understanding the role of academic and student affairs collaboration in creating a successful learning environment* (New Directions for Higher Education, no. 116, pp. 39–51). San Fransisco: Jossey-Bass.

Krueger, R. A. (1994). *Focus groups* (2nd ed.). Thousand Oaks, CA: Sage Publications.

Krueger, R. A. (1998). *Moderating focus groups: Focus group kit 4.* Thousand Oaks, CA: Sage Publications.

Kuh, G. D. (1996). Guiding principles for creating seamless learning environments for undergraduates. *Journal of College Student Development, 37* (2), 135–148.

Kuh, G. D., & Banta, T. W. (2000). Faculty-student affairs collaboration on assessment: Lessons from the field. *About Campus, 4* (6), 4–11.

Kuh, G. D., Douglas, K. B., Lund, J. P., & Ramin-Gyurnek, J. (1994). Student learning outside the classroom: Transcending artificial boundaries. *ASHE ERIC Higher Education Report,* no. 8. Washington, D.C.: The George Washington University, School of Education and Human Development.

LeCompte, M. D., & Preissle, J. (1993). *Ethnography and qualitative design in educational research* (2nd ed.). San Diego: Academic Press.

Lincoln, Y. S., & Guba, E. G. (1985). *Naturalistic inquiry.* Beverly Hills: Sage Publications.

Love, P. G., & Love, A. G. (1995). Enhancing student learning: Intellectual, social, and emotional integration. *ASHE-ERIC Higher Education Report, no. 4.* Washington, D.C.: George Washington University, Graduate School of Education and Human Development.

Maki, P. (2001). *Program review assessment.* Presentation to the Committee on Undergraduate Academic Program Review at North Carolina State University. Raleigh, North Carolina.

Maki, P. (2002). Moving from paperwork to pedagogy. *AAHE Bulletin* [Online]. Retrieved from http://www.aahebulletin.com/public/archive/paperwork.asp

Maki, P. (2003). Dialogue fuels assessment. *AAHE Inquiry and Action, 2.*

Marchese, T. J. (1998). Thinking about learning in relation to assessment: A conversation. Presentation at the American Association for Higher Education Assessment Conference, Cincinnati, OH.

Marshall, C., & Rossman, G. B. (1999). *Designing qualitative research* (3rd ed.). Thousand Oaks, CA: Sage Publications.

Maykut, P., and Morehouse, R. (1994). *Beginning qualitative research: A philosophic and practical guide.* London: The Falmer Press.

Mentkowski, M. (1998). Creating a culture of assessment: A look through the lens of assessment update: Assessment Trends: What have we learned from a decade of assessment? An Interactive Session at the American Association for Higher Education Assessment Conference, Cincinnati, OH.

Merriam, S. B. (1997). *Qualitative research and case study applications in education: Revised and expanded from case study research in education.* San Francisco: Jossey-Bass.

Merriam-Webster Online Dictionary. (2003). Retrieved from http://www.m-w.com/cgi-bin/dictionary

Miller, T. K. (Ed.). (1999). *The book of professional standards for higher education.* Washington, D.C.: Council for the Advancement of Standards in Higher Education.

Morante, E. A. (2002). *A handbook on assessment for two-year colleges.* Palm Desert, CA: College of the Desert, CA.

National Association of College and Employers. (1998). *Professional standards for college and university career services.* Bethlehem, PA: Author.

National Biological Service Carbrillo Tidepool Study [Online]. (2003). Retrieved from http://edweb.sdsu.edu/triton/tidepoolunit/Rubrics/collrubric.html

National Research Council. (2001). *Knowing what students know: The science and design of educational assessment.* Committee on the Foundations of Assessment. Washington, D.C.: National Academy Press.

Nichols, J. O. (1995). *A practitioner's handbook for institutional effectiveness and student outcomes assessment implementation* (3rd ed.). New York: Agathon Press.

North Carolina State University Committee on Undergraduate Program Review (CUPR). (2001a). *CUPR guidelines* [Online]. Retrieved from http://www.ncsu.edu/provost/governance /Ad_hoc/CUPR/

North Carolina State University Committee on Undergraduate Program Review (CUPR). (2001b). *CUPR common language* [Online]. Retrieved from http://www.ncsu.edu/provost/governance/ Ad_hoc/CUPR/

North Carolina State University Internet Resources for Higher Education Outcomes Assessment [Online]. (2003). Retrieved from http://www2.acs.ncsu.edu/UPA/assmt/resource.htm

Palomba, C. A., and Banta, T. W. (1999). *Assessment essentials: Planning, implementing, and improving assessment in higher education.* San Francisco: Jossey-Bass.

Patton, M. Q. (1989). *Qualitative evaluation methods (10th ed.).* Beverly Hills: Sage Publications.

Patton, P. Q. (2002). *Qualitative research and evaluation methods* (3rd ed.). Thousand Oaks, CA: Sage Publications.

Popham, W. J. (1997). What's wrong—and what's right—with rubrics. *Educational Leadership, 55* (2) [Online]. Retrieved from http://www.ascd.org/safeschools /el9710/pophamrubric.html

Schroeder, C. C., Blimling, G. S., McEwen, M. K., & Schuh, J. H. (Eds). (1996). The student learning imperative. *Journal of College Student Development, 37* (2). Washington, D.C.: American College Personnel Association.

Schuh, J. H., & Upcraft, M. L. (2001). *Assessment practice in student affairs: An application manual.* San Francisco: Jossey-Bass.

Seidman, I. (1998). *Interviewing as qualitative research: A guide for researchers in education and the social sciences.* New York: Teachers College Press.

Southern Association of Colleges and Schools. (2000). *Guidelines for accreditation* [Online]. Retrieved from http://www.sacscoc.org/

Spanbauer, S. (1996). *Reengineering education with quality.* Indianapolis, IN: USA Group Research Institute, 81–85.

Spendolini, M. J. (1992). *The benchmarking book.* New York: Amacom.

Stake, R. E. (1995). *The art of case study research.* Thousand Oaks, CA: Sage Publications.

Strauss, A., & Corbin, J. (1990). *Basics of qualitative research: Grounded theory procedures and techniques.* Newbury Park: Sage Publications.

Sybouts, W. (1992). *Planning in school administration: A handbook.* Westport, CT: Greenwood Press.

The Benchmarking Exchange. (2003). [Online]. Retrieved from http://www.benchnet.com

The Integrated Postsecondary Education Data System. (2003). *Integrated postsecondary education data system* [Online]. Retrieved from http://nces.ed.gov/ipeds/

The Psychological Corporation. (2003). Watson-Glaser Critical Thinking Appraisal [Online]. Retrieved from http://www.psychcorpcenter.com/content/wgct.htm

Trochim, W. M. (2002). *The research methods knowledge base* (2nd ed.) [Online]. Retrieved from http://trochim.human.cornell.edu/kb/index.htm

University of California, Los Angeles Higher Education Research Institute. (2003). Your First College Year [Online]. Retrieved from http://www.gseis.ucla.edu/heri/yfcy/survey_instrument.html

University of Victoria. (2003). *Bloom's taxonomy for professors* [Online]. Retrieved from http://www.coun.uvic.ca/learn/program/hndouts/bloom.html

Upcraft, M. L., & Schuh, J. H. (1996). *Assessment in student affairs: A guide for practitioners.* San Francisco: Jossey-Bass.

Whelchel, N. (2002). *Survey research* [Online]. A presentation for EAC 830 in fall 2003, North Carolina State University. Retrieved from http://www2.acs.ncsu.edu/UPA/survey/ uapr.survey_research/

BIBLIOGRAPHY

Alverno College. (2001a). *The diagnostic digital portfolio* [Online]. Retrieved from
    http://www.alverno.edu/ academics/ddp.html

Alverno College. (2001b). *Student assessment as learning and Alverno's eight abilities* [Online]. Retrieved from
    http://depts.alverno.edu/saal/

American College Health Association. (2001). Benchmarking surveys [Online]. Retrieved from
    http://www.acha.org/ projects_programs/datashare.cfm

American College Personnel Association. (2002). Assessment for Student Development Clearinghouse [Online].
    Retrieved from http://www.acpa.nche.edu/comms/ comm09/dragon/dragon-index.html

Council for the Advancement of Standards in Higher Education [Online]. (2003a). Retrieved from
    http://www.cas.edu

Council for the Advancement of Standards in Higher Education [Online]. (2003b). Retrieved from
    http://www.cas.edu/ faq.cfm

Creswell, J. W. (1998). *Qualitative inquiry and research design: Choosing among five traditions.*
    Thousand Oaks, CA: Sage Publications.

Dannells, M., & Lowery, J. W. (in press). Student discipline and judicial programs. In F. MacKinnon (Ed.),
    Student affairs practice in higher education (2nd ed.) Springfield, IL: Thomas.

Dodge, B. (2001). *Creating a rubric for a given task* [Online]. Retrieved from
    http://school.discovery.com /schrockguide/assess.html

ERIC Clearinghouse on Assessment and Evaluation [Online]. (1999–2003). Retrieved from http://ericae.net/

Helm, K. (2001). *Minutes from the committee on undergraduate academic program review* [Online]. Retrieved from
    http://www.ncsu.edu/provost/ governance/Ad_hoc/CUPR/

Holstein, J. A., and Grubrium, J. F. (1995). *The active interview.* Thousand Oaks, CA: Sage Publications.

Maki, P. (2002). Using multiple assessment methods to explore student learning and development inside and outside
    of the classroom. *NetResults* [Online]. Retrieved from http://www.naspa.org/

Pearson Education. (2001). *Electronic rubric example.* Upper Saddle River, NJ: Prentice-Hall.

San Diego Miramar College. (2003). *21st century learning outcomes project* [Online]. Retrieved from
    http://www.miramar.sdccd.net/ projects/league/index.asp

CPSIA information can be obtained at www.ICGtesting.com
Printed in the USA
BVOW050232100912

299945BV00002B/1/P